D0984753

DISCARDED

Jail Management

Jail Management

**Problems, Programs,
and Perspectives**

E. Eugene Miller

Lexington Books
D.C. Heath and Company
Lexington, Massachusetts
Toronto

Library of Congress Cataloging in Publication Data

Miller, E Eugene.
    Jail management.

    1. Prison administration—United States.
2. Prisons—United States. I. Title.
HV9469.M54   365'.973   76-43590
ISBN 0-669-00959-8

Second printing, June 1979.

Published simultaneously in Canada

Printed in the United States of America

International Standard Book Number: 0-669-00959-8

Library of Congress Catalog Card Number: 76-43590

This book is dedicated with enduring appreciation to the following five eminent penologists, whose patient tutoring, advice, and friendship have given me more knowledge of jails, the people incarcerated in them, and the people who run them than I could ever possibly absorb: John D. Case, Howard B. Gill, Kenneth L. Hardy, M. Robert Montilla, and James E. Murphy.

Contents

Acknowledgments

A very special thanks is also expressed to a true friend, Lady My, and to my mother, Loretta C. Miller, for their unswerving and continuing support and encouragement as well as to Louise Yescavage for her patience and diligence in preparing the manuscript.

Introduction

The warden of one of America's few truly progressive and effective jails once whimsically described his jail as a "shaggy dog." A more ingenious and accurate description of the contemporary jail in relation to other correctional institutions has not yet been devised. Architecturally foreboding and often inhumane, jails constitute the most forgotten and woebegone component of the criminal justice system.

Understandably, nobody seems to like jails—not the public that sends people to them and pays the bill, not the people who work in them, and definitely not the people confined in them. These local institutions stand as symbolic sentinels, attesting by their very existence to the human ills of a community. While statutorily established to hold people awaiting trial and, in many instances, to serve also as places of sentence for convicted people doing terms of less than one year, in human terms jails often function as dumping grounds for the unsightly and unwanted members of a community as well as detention facilities for the dangerous. In addition to actual or accused criminals, many such facilities are crammed with skid-row alcoholics, narcotics addicts, the mentally ill, and others whose "crimes" may be more unpleasant than threatening and who well may be more destructive of themselves than of others. Although jails are thus compelled to cater to a societal philosophy of "out of sight, out of mind," few people consider the fact that with an extreme paucity of exceptions, the inmates of these modern day asylums will eventually return to the community either less able or better prepared to cope with the realities and pressures of life in a dynamic environment.

The jail problem today is an unseemly tangle of unpedigreed components, i.e., public apathy, political and fiscal neglect, underqualified and untrained staff, among others, that simply will not disappear. Operating within such an unencouraging framework, almost miraculously there are some jails that through intelligent and innovative management, dedicated staffs, and the maximum utilization of community resources perform a valuable service to the communities they serve. While few in number, these local facilities evidence what can be accomplished even when far from ideal support is provided by government. Regrettably, the general picture of jails that emerges nationally is that of the most backward and neglected social institution in contemporary society.

The results of long-standing neglect are not difficult to imagine, even if they are somewhat unpalatable to admit. If Winston Churchill was right when he observed that "the sophistication of a society may be judged by the way in which it treats its prisoners," then the United States has not progressed very much in two centuries, despite landing men on the moon, achieving hitherto unimagined heights of affluence, and bequeathing the fast-food concept and cola beverages to the rest of the world.

In our country, there is a jail in which mentally disturbed people (*not* charged with any criminal offense) are kept in a totally dark room, shackled to a huge iron ring imbedded in the floor, pending transfer to a mental health facility—a process that may well take weeks to accomplish. There is a jail in which prisoners are kept in a subterranean unit, thus ensuring that they will never see natural light during their entire confinement. There are jails in which neglected and dependent children whose only "crimes" may be having parents who inflicted hideous physical abuse upon them are locked in cells with hardened criminals for playmates. What happens to women in some jails would shock and outrage even the more dedicated devotees of sadomasochism. No one will even hazard a guess as to the number of assaults and homosexual gang rapes that occurs in these facilities annually.

What makes the preceding picture even more disturbing is that most of the more than 1 million people who will pass through the nation's jails this year are being detained prior to trial. Many will eventually have their charges dismissed or be found innocent by a judge or jury. In many jurisdictions, the sole practical denominator between being locked up in a medieval, monkey-cage monstrosity or being free pending trial is the ability to pay a bondsman's fee.

Because of such deplorable conditions, the number of jails nationally (approximately 3921), the diversity of responsible governmental jurisdictions, the lack of sustained public interest in and commitment to remedial action, and myriad other problems, a growing number of penologists have abandoned the idea of jail reform, believing that an acceptable level of improvement cannot feasibly be attained. They propose as an alternative strategy the increased use of diversion, e.g., release on personal recognizance, third-party custody arrangements, participation in a variety of community-based helping programs as a mandatory condition of pretrial release. The advocates of diversion believe that many people now confined do not need to be incarcerated to ensure public safety and that diversion is both cheaper and more cost-effective than institutionalization. Consequently, some might argue that any serious attempt to improve jails is self-defeating in that it would channel off resources and energies that could better be used to create a significant system of alternatives to incarceration.

Diversion is certainly worthy of intensive and immediate exploration and initiatives. Similarly, the whole issue of meaningful bail reform, which would alleviate the injustices of the present system while providing for public safety, should be the subject of significant consideration and action. However, the public's lack of recognition and/or understanding of these problems and its deep-seated antipathy to any measure that even remotely appears to be a softening of legal strictures militate against the creation of a political climate in the foreseeable future that would be receptive to these laudatory and overdue improvements. Meanwhile, more than 1 million people annually are exposed to the current system of jail incarceration in which the only rational individual goal is sheer survival. Given the demonstrable potential of jails to harm such a substantial number of people, prudent, relevant steps must be taken to improve jails at least to the point at which they would no longer be institutions of debilitation. However desirable diversion may be, the local jail will remain a primary mode of dealing with pretrial and short-term offenders for many years.

It is not the purpose of this book to chronicle the many documentable horror stories emanating from municipal and county jails. Occasional media exposés and a variety of first-person and investigative reportage books have sufficiently covered that topic, with little lasting impact upon day-to-day operations. Instead, the objectives of this book are to provide the college student who is interested in a career in criminal justice with an introduction to and understanding of the jail problem in the United States and to give the worker in the field and interested citizens some pragmatic suggestions for effecting immediate improvements.

Ironically, the resources necessary to accomplish the task of jail reform exist in virtually every community in the country and frequently lie within the potentials of the institution's existing staff, if they are properly organized, trained, and directed. Identification and appropriate utilization of available community services and the adoption of modern managerial techniques are far more vital to the achievement of the goal than is a massive infusion of new funds, except in the more extreme cases. While increased budgetary support is, of course, highly desirable, jail managers and citizens can still affect marked improvements in the system, for the ultimate determinant of a good jail is the human dimension, i.e., management, staff dedication, number and quality of inmate interactions with staff and community, and other similar factors. The physical structure of a particular institution may help or hinder such efforts, but certainly does not in any instance prevent or prohibit them.

Currently, a matrix of forces is combining to assert pressure to affect at least some measure of reform. Perhaps foremost among these is the substantial amount of civil litigation questioning certain jail practices and procedures. Increasingly, inmates are successfully suing jails and responsible units of local government for negligence resulting in personal injury from assaults, homosexual rapes, and similar untoward occurrences. Several public interest legal groups have brought sweeping class action suits, seeking, and in some instances obtaining, major changes in intolerable conditions. The U.S. Department of Justice recently has also taken an activist role and has recently initiated legal action to alleviate cruel and unusual conditions of confinement and to eliminate racial segregation in several major jails in various regions of the country. While temporary political pressures can be stonewalled and the best intentions of citizen reform groups can be dissipated in a maze of bureaucracy, court orders and substantial monetary awards for damages cannot be ignored.

Several states have established commissions to consider the formulation of mandatory minimum qualifications for local law enforcement and correctional personnel—a necessary, long overdue, first step in the upgrading of the criminal justice process. An increasing number of state legislatures are establishing minimum standards for the operation of local jails. The Commission on Accreditation for Corrections, a private organization originally sired by the American Correctional Association, is about to launch a national self-evaluation effort for all types of correctional agencies, including jails. The National Institute of Corrections, an agency within the U.S. Department of Justice, adopted the improvement of local facilities as a major thrust of its training efforts for fiscal year 1977. The National Sheriffs' Association has also made several attempts in recent years to improve facility management by expanding the knowledge base of its membership, which administers approximately 85 percent of all jails nationally.

In addition, a growing number of citizens' groups are being formed with the avowed purpose of improving local institutions. Inmates themselves have become significantly more aware of their rights. Several ex-offender groups around the nation are making a substantial contribution to jail reform both through public education efforts and by providing needed post release services to former clients of the system.

Fragmented and, in some instances, token as many of these efforts may be, they nonetheless represent positive action on many fronts toward the attainment of the reform objective. It is essential now to increase, mobilize, and sustain the interest of these diverse parties and to educate the public and correctional workers alike concerning both the urgent need for improvement and the pragmatic means by which to achieve it.

The end goal of such efforts is not to turn jails into resort hotels, as some reactionaries have not so subtly suggested. Rather it is to ensure that the men and women confined in local correctional institutions are treated fairly and humanely in an atmosphere that is conducive to fostering meaningful rehabilitative activities while providing for public safety. Ultimately, progressive jail management is primarily victim oriented by recognizing that successful intervention at an early stage of a criminal career prevents future crimes. Currently prevailing conditions merely serve to embitter, not correct—to foster criminal activity, not prevent it. In the cases of people who are in fact innocent, detained and awaiting trial, it is an abominable indictment of the system that they are likely to emerge from the jail experience far worse off than when they entered. Hence, a well managed jail has the potential of being a positive asset to a community by having an impact upon both the local crime problem and the quality of justice.

This book provides an overview of the contemporary American jail and addresses the major aspects of jail operation with a view to their improvement. It is well to remember that there is no single answer to the jail problem, just as there is no single answer to the correction of those forms of deviant behavior which are defined by society as criminal. However, there are approaches that, when modified to meet local conditions and needs, can lead to vast improvement. Since crime is the result of a combination of disparate elements embedded deeply in the interactions of a particular individual with a given community, no jail can perform its task effectively unless it is perceived as being an integral part of the locality it serves. This concept makes it imperative to convert the traditional lockup into a community correctional center, if the jail is to have a valid and valued role in a modern criminal justice system.

1 Overview of American Jails

We shouldn't treat cattle the way we have to house our inmates.

Anna M. Kross

The jail is old, dirty, and poorly run. The inmates are surly and show no respect or even fear of jail personnel. Supervision of inmate activity is of the most minimal kind as is the staffing of the jail. Inmates were dirty and smelly as were their cells. . . . Inmate abuse of other inmates probably runs pretty much unchecked since at no time during the tour did I encounter any guards supervising or checking an area.

Hans W. Mattick and Ronald P. Sweet

One prison official, ashamed and offended, referred to the dormitories as "the Black Hole of Calcutta."

Ronald Goldfarb

Welcome to the typical American jail—decrepit; underfunded; with too few and untrained, underqualified employees; temporary home to over 1 million people a year (many of them legally innocent); and key element in the criminal justice process. Exaggerated? Unfortunately not, although there are some notably positive exceptions. The sad truth is that too few people seem to know or care about what really happens in jails, unless they are unlucky enough to be in one. If, as Philadelphia's Mayor Frank Rizzo is fond of saying, "a conservative is a liberal who was mugged the night before," then surely a jail reformer is virtually anyone who has ever spent a night behind bars.

Within a given state, the quality and conditions of jails can vary greatly from county to county, for with few exceptions, jails are a wholly local responsibility and reflect the attitudes, philosophy, revenue base, and similar social, economic, and political factors found in a given community. Hence, it is quite possible to visit a jail that is a paragon of progressive correctional practice, only to drive a few minutes, cross a jurisdictional line, and encounter a hellhole in the next town or county. Most frequently, however, such personal forays into the correctional landscape result in the discovery of uniformly atrocious facilities that differ only in the specifics of the inhuman conditions and degree of poor management therein.

1

Neither this chapter nor this book as a whole are intended to present a sensationalistic view of the jail problem. The recitation of horror stories concerning local correctional facilities has been accomplished on many occasions and in many locales by the media and by various first-person articles and books. The difficulty with such approaches to reform is that their impact upon the reader is transitory and no solutions that recognize the real underlying causes of problems within the system are presented. The so-called first television generation, which grew up in the 1950s, was constantly exposed to Sergeant Friday's clarion call for "The facts, M'am, just the facts" on "Dragnet." Hence, this chapter, as an overview, will present a purely factual depiction of American jails.

Definition

As used in this book, a *jail* is an institution administered by a local unit of government that has the authority to detain adults for a period of 48 hours or longer.[1] In various locales, these facilities may also be known as detention centers, county prisons, workhouses, or houses of correction. This definition specifically excludes overnight lockups, which are frequently found in city police stations or precinct houses. The latter are not considered herein, since their only function is to hold people for a very brief period prior to an initial court appearance, at which time the individuals will either be released on bail or personal recognizance or remanded to a jail for purposes of further detention or incarceration.

Functions

Within the criminal justice system, jails serve three primary functions. First, they detain people awaiting trial who have not been able to post bail or secure release either on personal recognizance or by some sort of court approved third-party custody arrangement. In medium-sized or small municipalities and counties, jails may also perform the overnight detention function, which is usually performed by the police in the large, urban jurisdictions. Second, jails are the institutions in which convicted people sentenced to a term of less than one year (misdemeanants) serve their time. In several states, under certain specified conditions, jails may also be the place of sentence for long-term offenders (felons), but this practice is not common. Third, jails also hold individuals who have been convicted but not yet sentenced by the courts. Similarly, newly convicted felons are frequently confined in jails pending transfer to a state prison. One additional function, which, because of its nature, is not performed very often, is the holding of material witnesses to ensure their appearance in court or their personal safety prior to testifying.

Contemporary social philosophy, sound correctional practice, and common sense mandate that juveniles who require detention prior to the disposition of their cases by the juvenile court be kept in appropriate, separate facilities established specifically for this purpose. Even if jails could guarantee total separation of juvenile from adult prisoners, the unique needs of youngsters and the exigencies of the juvenile justice system (a totally different and separate system than that for adults, with its own governing statutes, rules, and procedures) call for an entirely different type of facility in virtually every way. While in some areas jails do serve in fact as detention centers for juveniles, the practice is considered somewhat barbaric and not an appropriate function for a jail to assume.

Many small and medium-sized communities also use jails as de facto dumping grounds for any type of deviant or problem individual. For example, it is not unusual for a mentally disturbed person who is either manifesting or threatening disruptive behavior (which is not necessarily criminal) to be confined in jail pending some other disposition, which may take days, weeks, or, in some instances, months to finalize. Similarly, until relatively recent court decisions and enlightened legislation in some states prohibited the practice, chronic alcoholics, usually having been charged with public drunkenness, crowded jails throughout the nation in astronomical numbers. These people did not pose a danger to public safety, but were unwanted eyesores. Still today, in many areas, detention facilities serve as massive "drunk tanks."

Such practices are evidence of the failure of some local governments to provide appropriate, alternative resources and facilities for these types of people either through deliberate neglect or, in the case of many rural jurisdictions, because of a tax base too inadequate to support a full spectrum of services. Yet jails are neither equipped nor properly staffed to meet the special needs of people whose primary problems or "offenses" are of a physical or mental health nature. Nevertheless, jails cannot legally refuse to accept these people if they are committed under proper procedure. This dumping-ground function exists in practice, if not in theory, and constitutes a unique problem for conscientious jail managers. In reality, all these managers can do is to call public attention to the problem and hope that the local government will make an attempt to live up to its responsibility in this area, while simultaneously utilizing whatever resources they can develop in an effort to cope with the very real human problem at hand.

Objectives

Jails exist to *enhance public safety* by keeping in secure custody those people who are deemed a criminal threat to other people or property and to en-

sure that people awaiting court action appear for trial. In everyday operation, this translates into the prevention of escapes and the maintenance of
order within the institution. That segment of operational policies and procedures designed to achieve this objective is referred to as "security."

Jails are also expected to effect some measure of positive behavioral
and/or attitudinal change on the part of the offender, i.e., to *rehabilitate*
him or her. As a practical matter, a large number of jail administrators view
this objective as either inappropriate or decidedly secondary in nature to
that of public safety. Yet professional organizations such as the American
Correctional Association, the National Sheriffs' Association, and the National Jail Association, as well as such recently established bodies as the National Advisory Commission on Criminal Justice Standards and Goals and
the President's (Johnson) Commission on Law Enforcement and the Administration of Justice, view rehabilitation as a proper and major concern
of jails.

If a criminal offender were merely confined for a given period of time,
then ultimately public safety would not be served, since the individual in all
likelihood would revert to unlawful conduct upon release because of a lack
of attempted intervention into his or her behavioral patterns. In a very real
sense, jails can contribute to a short-term achievement of public safety by
the very act of incarceration; but a long-term contribution to the reduction
of crime mandates the successful accomplishment of the rehabilitation objective.

Punishment is another very real objective of a jail. For a time, this concept fell out of fashion in polite conversation; but recently, it has returned
in the form of a criminological "insight." Short of the death penalty,
deprivation of liberty is the most serious punishment that a democracy can
impose. Forced separation from society in combination with the isolation
and hyperregimentation that are facts of life in any institution constitute
punishment by any rational definition.

Therefore, incarceration in and of itself is a major form of punishment.
Odious conditions within an institution and such "programs" as having inmates wash floors with toothbrushes or dig ditches only to refill and redig
them (an activity seriously recommended to me by a then member of Congress in open committee sessions) serve no valid purposes other than to embitter offenders and are thus wholly counterproductive to the attainment of
the rehabilitation objective. The sage observation that "an individual is in
prison as punishment, not for punishment" places this objective in its proper perspective.[2]

Types of Jails

There are three basic types of jails. The first is the *detention* jail, which is
used solely to confine people awaiting trial. There is also the *sentenced* jail,

wherein misdemeanants serve out their sentences as imposed by the court. Separate detention and sentenced jails are rarely found outside of large, metropolitan areas, primarily because of cost considerations based on the number of people confined. A third type of jail is the combined *detention-sentenced* facility, wherein all county or city prisoners are housed. This is by far the most common type of facility nationally.

Administrative Framework

Jails are a responsibility of local government. Within that framework, approximately 85 percent of these institutions are administered by sheriffs, for whom operation of the jail is a task added to their primary law enforcement duties. Currently there is a minor trend developing to establish a distinct local agency, usually called a Department of Corrections, to administer county and/or municipal jails. Several major cities, such as New York and Washington, D.C., have long had such arrangements, as have a few counties, Westchester (N.Y.) being a prime example. In jurisdictions in which neither a sheriff nor a separate department has the responsibility, the local unit of government hires an administrator (warden or superintendent) to operate the facility. Next to having the jail under the aegis of the sheriff, this latter mode is still more prevalent than is the city or county department of corrections.

The Federal Bureau of Prisons has its own jails in San Diego, Chicago, and New York (called Metropolitan Correctional Centers) to hold people awaiting trial in federal courts and is in the process of constructing similar facilities in other metropolitan areas. In places where there are federal courts but no federal detention capability the Bureau of Prisons contracts with the local jail for the care and custody of federal pretrial prisoners. Currently there are approximately 800 of these contracts in force.

In Alaska, Connecticut, Delaware, Hawaii, Rhode Island, and Vermont the state corrections agency also is responsible for administering some or all of the local jails.

Standards and Inspections

There are no mandatory federal standards, other than the general provisions of the Constitution, that must be complied with in the operation of jails. While a variety of national and presidential commissions have made recommendations and proposed model standards and goals in this area, there is no compulsory obligation on the part of the local governmental units to adopt them. The Federal Bureau of Prisons occasionally will inspect certain jails, but only for the purpose of determining their adequacy and appropriateness for holding federal prisoners on the aforementioned contractual basis.

Thirty-two states have established minimum standards for jail operation and have instituted mechanisms for inspection and enforcement. In a few states where this inspection function is adequately staffed with knowledgeable people whose findings and recommendations are backed up by the appropriate state officials, some improvement has been noted. In other states, however, there are too few inspectors and many of them are either unqualified or are prone to establish too close relationships with jail administrators as a means of ensuring their own job security. A recommendation to close or effect marked improvements in a jail because of a prevalence of intolerable and uncorrected conditions can bring forth substantial political pressures on legislators and other state officials from the jurisdiction concerned. These pressures often result in the inspection report being conveniently forgotten or amended from above. However, by having the power to close a jail, even if it is politically unfeasible to do so, inspectors in a few states have been able to convince certain jurisdictions to upgrade jail facilities and operations.

A number of organizations and commissions have promulgated standards and recommendations for jail operation. The American Correctional Association, the National Advisory Commission on Criminal Justice Standards and Goals, and the National Sheriffs' Association, among others, have developed and issued reasonable guidelines,[3] any one of which, if implemented on a large-scale basis, would result in considerable improvements. The United Nations has also established minimum rules for the treatment of offenders.[4] Although formally approved and issued by that international body in 1955, some two decades later only Pennsylvania, South Carolina, Ohio, Minnesota, Connecticut, and Illinois had adopted them.[5] Of these six states, only Connecticut made any specific provision to apply them to local jails as well as to state prisons. No individual jail anywhere in the nation has taken the initiative to adopt and implement these minimum international guidelines.

The Commission on Accreditation for Corrections, a private organization located in Rockville, Maryland, is about to launch a national self-evaluation and accreditation effort for correctional agencies, including jails. While participation in this effort by institutions is strictly voluntary, such a project marks an important first step in establishing an objective means for evaluating an individual facility with reference to an objective national standard. Established practice for many other types of social institutions, such as hospitals, schools, colleges, and universities, a system of accreditation in corrections is a long overdue necessity.

Number and Size

At midyear 1972, the most recent year for which reliable national statistics are available, there were 3921 jails in the United States.[6] On the day on which this computation was made, these jails confined 141,588 inmates, an average of 36 per institution. It should be noted, however, that because of the high turnover in jails, which is concomitant with their function as short-term institutions, the actual number of people confined during an entire year easily exceeds 1 million. Of the total number of jails, roughly three out of four (2901) house 20 or fewer inmates; 907 facilities are medium sized, having between 21 and 249 "residents"; the other 113 jails (3 percent of the total) have inmate populations of 250 or more.

Location and Size

Of all jails, 48 percent (1865) are located in the South. The Midwest has 1153 such facilities, followed by the West with 672 and the Northeast with 231. In examining the average number of inmates per jail, however, the picture is somewhat reversed. In the Northeast there were 118 inmates per facility, as contrasted with the West with 52, the South with 30, and the Midwest with 20. On a state-by-state basis, Texas has the most jails (318), followed by Georgia (239), Florida (164), Ohio (161), and California (152).

These marked contrasts between regions relative to the number and size of jails may be accounted for by differences in population density, historical development of political subdivisions, state laws, local philosophies and attitudes toward the criminal offender, and widely divergent practices in the courts.

Characteristics of the People in Confinement

Approximately 95 percent of the people confined in local jails nationally are males.[7] Of the total jail population, roughly 25 percent are between 21 and 24 years old, and fully a half are in the 19 to 29 age group. A disproportionate 42 percent of all inmates are black, while 56 percent are white, and the remaining 2 percent are members of other racial groups, primarily American Indian and Oriental.

About 25 percent of all confinees had no more than an eighth grade education. Another 40 percent were high school dropouts or kickouts. Approximately 10 percent had at least attended some sort of college, while another 25 percent had graduated from high school but had not pursued any further formal education.

At the time of their commitment to jail, approximately 40 percent of the inmates had been unemployed—about 30 percent, in fact, had been out of work for more than a year. Of those with jobs, 20 percent were only working part-time; 55 percent had annual incomes of less than $3000 during the year prior to commitment; another 31 percent had earned between $3000 and $7499; while the remaining 14 percent had incomes in excess of $7500.

These figures are based upon a 1972 survey, a year in which the median income in the United States was $9255.

Approximately 75 percent of the people being held in jail awaiting trial were there because they were unable to post the amount of bail set by the court. Twenty-five percent had been denied bail altogether. "Given the custodial purposes of incarceration for drunkenness and vagrancy, it was not surprising that the highest rates of bail denial involved these misdemeanor-type offenses."[8] In other words, the least dangerous offenders had a greater likelihood of being incarcerated prior to trial than did people posing serious threats to the safety of the community.

Furthermore, several federal courts have ruled that a chronic alcoholic cannot be charged with public intoxication under a criminal statute since he or she is involuntarily manifesting a symptom of a recognized disease and is, consequently, a public health problem, not a criminal problem. Hence, depending on the specific jurisdiction, a chronic alcoholic in one area may be left alone or civilly committed to an appropriate public health facility for treatment; in another, he or she may be incarcerated in jail with bail denied—in a criminal justice version of spin the bottle.

On average, a person confined awaiting trial will spend at least three months in jail.

Physical Plants

Roughly 60 percent of all jails share the use of their building with other functions, e.g., the county courthouse, sheriff's office, or local police station. Inside a majority of jails, several types of accommodations are to be found. These include some combination of one-, two-, three-, or four-inmate cells and dormitories.

The differences in types of inmate housing are significant. One-inmate cells provide for greater privacy and security. At the other extreme, four-inmate cells increase the possibility of several cellmates ganging up on another and, hence, in a well-run jail, mandate careful screening and assignment of individuals to specific quarters.

Dormitories usually house minimum security inmates and "trustees" and are far less expensive to construct and maintain because floor space is more efficiently used and steel bars and steel-reinforced concrete walls (such equipment frequently constitutes 15 to 20 percent of initial construction costs) are held to a minimum. However, in dormitories, the space involved, the freer inmate movement, the use of double bunk beds in the event of overcrowding, and similar factors serve to reduce effective supervision by the guards. The use of dormitories should be accompanied by an effective screening and assignment process. Presuming proper assignment procedures, inmates often prefer dormitories as being less oppressive and constricting than security cells.

Approximately 44 percent of jails have a drunk tank. These "tanks" are either very large cells or quasi-dormitories in which drunks are put to sober up. A well-equipped drunk tank will have heat, light, ventilation, beds or mattresses (soil resistant types that can be sterilized easily are available), toilets, and drinking spouts. In actual fact, very few jails provide all these facilities. Nineteen jails provide none of them at all; 7 percent do not make light and heat available; 14 percent have no toilets; 50 percent do not even provide a place, other than the floor, to sit down; 26 percent have no window or fan. It takes little imagination to conceive of the aroma emanating from a room with no ventilation or toilets after a night's use by a score of inebriates.

A number of communities have followed the lead of St. Louis, Missouri in providing sleep-off and detoxification centers in lieu of incarceration and criminal prosecution of intoxicated people. This approach is not only a civilized alternative to drunk tanks, but also greatly reduces the workload of the local courts and the overcrowding of jail facilities. Regrettably, there are no national statistics available by which to gauge objectively such factors as average age of jails, overcrowding, and adequacy and condition of physical plants. Occasionally a fatal fire or similar tragedy in a jail will be reported by the media, with subsequent investigation often pointing up faulty design or improper maintenance. It is impossible to tell with certainty the number of jails in which vermin; inadequate plumbing, lighting, and ventilation; and fire hazards abound.

A number of jails still in use (precisely how many cannot be determined) were opened prior to the Civil War. In fact, I have visited one county jail that originally served as a Hessian guard house during the Revolutionary War. I have also been in two jails in which the inmate housing units are entirely below ground, with no possibility of any natural light seeping in—both institutions as a matter of policy rarely allow the majority of inmates to emerge from these areas. While some conditions discovered in local facilities would be revolting to knowledgeable correctional officials, none would be surprising.

Food Service

Approximately 70 percent of jails serve food prepared in the jail, while the others make arrangements to have food brought in. Two jails make no provisions whatever to feed the people in confinement. The specific arrangements are, in large part, dependent upon the size of the institution, with the larger facilities generally doing their own food preparation. Seven institutions (all small) provide only one meal per day; roughly one-third have two meals, and, the other two-thirds serve three meals. Again, the larger the institution, the greater the probability that three meals a day are served. With the exception of 45 jails, at least one hot meal a day is provided.

These figures relate only to frequency of food service and give no indication of quantity, quality, or nutritional adequacy. Withour fear of contradiction, however, it can be stated that the *chez prison* would not be the dining establishment of choice for very many citizens. This is not to advocate that food service in jails should reflect the best in *haute cuisine*, but that steps should be taken to ensure that meals served should be ample in quantity, wholesome, nutritious, and certainly more than minimally palatable. Observance of this standard alone would be a marked improvement for most of the nation's jails and lead to a noticeable uplifting of inmate morale and overall health.

Medical Services

An inhouse medical area of some type can be found in 12.5 percent of local jails. However, this does not necessarily imply the availability of beds, since an "area" can be little more than an examining room or nurse's office. Of the large city jails, 60 percent do have infirmaries. Infirmaries are critical in a jail, if people with infectious (including venereal) diseases are to be separated from other inmates and staff, in addition to being necessary for many other medical purposes.

The lack of adequate medical care is perhaps most strikingly evidenced by the fact that only 19 percent (744) of jails in the United States have a doctor. These institutions employ 1063 physicians, but only 34 percent of them serve on a full-time basis. In five states, there are no nurses whatever on jail staffs. Such a staffing alignment not only indicates the lack of proper diagnosis and treatment of illness, but also effectively rules out all but the most cursory of physical examinations upon commitment—even this preliminary check is, in most cases, performed by a guard, not a medical professional.

Classification

Classification is the term used to denote the categorization of offenders by various criteria for the purposes of making housing assignments, determining security status, and developing rehabilitation programs. In its most rudimentary form, classification entails the separation of inmates by sex, age (juvenile, adult), and legal status (pretrial or detention, sentenced).

There is no known jail that fails to house women apart from men. However, given the absence of physical examinations at the time of admission and certain contemporary grooming and fashion styles, such mixing of the sexes has occurred in rare instances. In one case, a very slender woman was housed in a cellblock with male prisoners for several weeks and failed to make known her sexual identity for fear of possible sexual abuse by other inmates or staff. It was not until her transfer to a more progressive jail that this situation became known and immediately remedied.

Seventy-nine jails mix their adult and juvenile prisoners, which is a direct violation of law in a number of states in which this practice is found. Included in this number are large jails in Missouri, Ohio, and Pennsylvania. Such administrative cretinism should not be tolerated or condoned by any community, and firm, corrective action should be taken at once to rectify it.

Because of their immaturity, dependency, potential vulnerability, and special needs, juveniles should not be held in jails. Rather, separate detention facilities, properly designed and staffed, should be established. This is especially true when one considers that many juveniles are being detained pending juvenile court disposition on "status" offenses, i.e., acts that if committed by an adult would not be considered illegal. Running away from home, truancy, and violation of curfew are several of the "status" offenses. The potential harm and corruption that might befall juveniles were they to be confined in jails is sufficiently obvious that most states have specifically outlawed this abominable practice. If separate juvenile detention facilities do not exist in a particular jurisdiction, under no conceivable circumstances should juveniles be mixed with adults in a jail, but rather they should be kept separated in a distinct wing or unit.

In combined detention-sentenced jails, proper administration would ensure that pretrial prisoners are separated from those who have already been convicted. The difference in legal status implicitly demands a less punitive approach toward pretrial detainees, who are still considered legally innocent of any crime. Thus, for example, detention prisoners cannot be compelled to work and should have greater access to appropriate means of contact with the community to ensure proper preparation of a legal defense. This is not to say, however, that proper security and other precautions should not be employed to prevent escapes and maintain order within the detention part of the jail. Yet 2011 jails freely mix pretrial and sentenced inmates, thus patently ignoring a fundamental tenet of the American criminal justice system.

Two hundred and forty jails do not even separate seriously mentally ill people from the general inmate population. Included in that number are two large jails in Texas and one each in Arizona, California, Florida, and Missouri.

Americans tend to believe that they are exceptionally fair in their consideration and treatment of others, especially those who might be considered "underdogs." Hence, you may automatically assume that if the foregoing figures relative to the rudimentary elements of classification indicate that American jails fail to observe the most basic standards in this area, either the standards are somehow unfair or, in any event, certainly no other country in the world abides by them either. Of 58 countries whose correctional practices were explored in 1975, 36 had fully implemented the United Nations standards concerning the separation of prisoners—standards that are more stringent than those alluded to in this section.[9] In many instances, serious assaults, homosexual rapes, escapes, and other dangerous acts that occur too frequently in jails can be directly traced to the failure to establish and implement proper classification practices and procedures.

Recreational Facilities

Just over 60 percent of all jails make some type of recreation or entertainment available to inmates. No such provisions whatever are made by 1495 jails. Some sort of constructive outlet and physical exercise are absolutely necessary for the maintenance of both physical and mental health. This lack of recreational opportunity, even if it is only the availability of a radio or television set, in combination with the pervasive idleness found in most jails leads to an escalation of tension and increased incidents of violence in addition to the mental and physical deterioration of the people confined.

Staffing

Jails employ 44,293 people, of whom 89 percent are full-time workers. On the average, large institutions have 145 employees (both full and part time), compared to 17 in medium-sized facilities, and 4 in the small jails. Custodial personnel (guards) comprise 46 percent of the total employed; administrative staff makes up another 27 percent; 17 percent perform clerical or maintenance functions; and the remaining 10 percent are principally specialists, e.g,. physicians. Of these specialists, 40 percent are employed part-time, however, compared to only 7 percent of those in the other categories combined.

Further analysis of the specialist category reveals that only 114 jails retain the services of a phychiatrist. Of the 166 psychiatrists so employed, approximately 75 percent are part-time. Only 95 jails have a staff psychologist. Of the 137 psychologists working in these institutions, 50 percent are employed on a part-time status. Four hundred and eighty-two social workers (one-third part-timers) are on the staffs of 182 jails. Academic teachers are found in 136 jails (3 percent of the total). In 21 states, not even one jail employed a teacher. Seventy-eight jails have vocational instructors—a figure that is suspicious, since often vocational teachers have some degree of responsibility for institution maintenance and the instruction function tends to be viewed as secondary to other duties. No jail in 22 states has a vocational instructor.

Rehabilitation Programs

While very few jails commit budgetary resources to the establishment and operation of programs, a number have used federal funds for this purpose. For the most part, however, these funds are nonrenewable past the third year of a given grant award; and hence, if the programs are to be continued, their costs must be assumed eventually by the local jurisdiction. Two-thirds of all jails with programs rely solely on community volunteers for the actual provision of such services.

Six hundred and seventy-eight jails have some type of group counseling; 419 offer remedial education; another 542 provide vocational training (most often through a federal manpower program); and 226 make prevocational testing available. There are no statistics that would indicate the quality of these programs, however, nor the number of inmate participants. This consideration becomes highly relevant when one recognizes, for example, that without skilled leadership, group counseling in name often deteriorates to bull sessions in practice.

By far the most predominant program in jails is religious services. Nearly 60 percent of local institutions have this activity, which is conducted usually by either volunteer members of the local ministerium or church lay groups. Some organizations, such as the Salvation Army, also provide substantial assistance to inmates by way of informal counseling and help in securing employment and adequate lodging upon release. Other community groups, such as Alcoholics Anonymous, often actively offer services to people with more particular problems in many of the nation's jails.

Work Release

Work release is a program that enables sentenced offenders to hold jobs in the community during the day, returning to the institution at night. Usually, the participants pay a small sum to the jail as reimbursement for room and board. Among the major advantages of work release are that the inmate immediately becomes a taxpayer instead of a tax-user and gradually becomes readjusted to life in the free community.

Work release is available in 42 percent (1665) of all jails, which is one of the few bright signs in the jail administration field. As usual, there are no figures available to indicate either the success of such efforts or the extent of offender participation. Since work release has been a widely accepted correctional technique in this country for only a decade (most states passed the appropriate enabling legislation in the middle and late 1960s), there is reason to expect that more jails will implement such programs in the near future. Work release is relatively inexpensive to operate and conveys many benefits to the offender and to the community. Its ultimate success, however, depends on the quality of screening, i.e., classification, of the inmate/applicants; and this, as has already been noted, is a very weak area in jail management.

Costs

Precisely accurate cost and expenditure data are not available for jails nationwide. However, by utilizing the comprehensive staffing, program, and offender information for the most recent year for which such statistics are available, i.e., 1972, and combining these with survey information for the same period relating to overall costs and expenditures of the criminal justice system, some relevant figures can be arrived at with reasonable confidence. The estimates that follow are expressed in 1974 dollars.

It costs approximately $5721 to keep one inmate in jail for a year. Other than vocational training and education, this figure does not reflect any expenditures for rehabilitation activities. Examining the specific components of the overall average annual per-inmate incarceration costs, custody and basic support services, including provisions for basic human needs, account for $3874 of the total.[10] The provision of some educational and vocational training activities costs an average of $1337.[11] Costs related to counseling, therapy, recreation, and similar programs would, if available, add to the expenditure total.

To ensure proper custody and supervision in a correctional facility, a generally accepted standard is that there should be one guard on the staff for every six inmates. This figure is not as high as it would first appear if one remembers that a jail is a 24-hour-per-day operation, normally requiring three 8-hour shifts of custodial employees, and that these personnel are also frequently used to transport inmates to and from courts, medical facilities outside the institution, and so on. The achievement of this basic standard would require an additional expenditure of $42.5 million for salaries and fringe benefits *only*—uniforms, training, and other such employee-related expenses would be extra. Expressed in annual per-inmate terms, this would result in an additional expenditure of $345.[12]

Should it become either desirable or necessary to build a new facility, again considerable funds are involved. The average construction costs for new jails opened between 1973 and 1976 (average opening date of 1974) was $27,432 per bed.[13] Thus it would take $6,858,000 to build a new jail with a capacity of 250. These figures, of course, do not include any additional operating or staffing costs.

In addition to the direct operational and capital costs of jails, there are also considerable "indirect" costs. These would include the cost of individual crimes to the victims; expenses of the criminal justice system in investigation, apprehension, prosecution, and sentencing; public assistance payments to inmates' dependents; tax revenues lost because of the offenders' inability to work while incarcerated; and many other similar, very real economic losses experienced by the community.

Unfortunately, figures that would be sufficiently comprehensive to permit more than a wildly crude guess about these costs simply do not exist in any remotely reliable form. However, a reasonably accurate estimate has been made of the productivity loss (primarily based upon assumed salary figures and similar inputs) entailed by society in the process of confining people in jail. On an annual basis, this loss is calculated to be $972 million. This assumes an unemployment rate of 15 percent, were the inmates to be in the community, and gives productivity credit for institutional maintenance work performed by offenders while incarcerated.[14]

Conclusions

Jails currently constitute a very expensive form of human warehousing. Even worse, if rehabilitation efforts are neither tried nor successful, one may reasonably anticipate a recurrence of these costs and expenditures in the cases of individual offenders. When these dollar costs are combined with the human costs associated with the neglect frequently cited elsewhere, the inevitable question is: Can this country continue to afford the luxury of a jail system that accomplishes little more than the quite temporary segregation of offenders from the community, if that?

An anonymous wit once observed that "Crime wouldn't pay, if the government ran it." The depressing fact is that, currently, crime pays extremely well, while the investment in crime control measures, including jails, escalates with few apparent dividends to society. It is about time that the ledger be reversed.

2 Components of the Problem

There ain't no votes in prison.

Huey Long

There are myriad reasons why jails are in their current dolorous condition. Some of these are rooted deeply in history; others result from a broad range of current socioeconomic factors. Some are obvious, while still more require an intimate knowledge of the criminal justice process to be perceived and fully comprehended. No single chapter could possibly contain a complete listing of the many factors underlying the utter failure of America's jails and the continuing human tragedy which that failure represents. This chapter, however, will present some of the more salient components of the jail problem.

Public Apathy

About the only time that jails are mentioned in the typical American household is when little Johnny does something particularly odious and his parents wish to scare him out of a repeat performance, i.e., "If you do that again, I'll call the policeman and he'll come and take you to jail." The same proscribed conduct still occurs, of course, only the child becomes more surreptitious about it—an interesting lesson in the adult game of "It's only wrong, if you get caught." Aside from that, an occasional "You might have known that *he'd* never serve a day in jail" is one of the rare allusions to the local correctional facility made by most citizens.

The psychological processes involved in this oversight are quite simple to detect. Since jails are not particularly pleasant places nor the people confined therein especially congenial, "out of sight, out of mind" is a convenient way to pretend that they do not even exist. Consider what transpires when a sensationalistic crime occurs in a community. Virtually everyone rushes to read or view the sordid details unveiled ad nauseam in the media. The community is shocked, outraged, even titillated. Interest continues through the trial and possibly even to the day of sentencing. After that, convinced that the criminal has gotten his or her just desserts, no one is interested anymore. Since the offender is effectively segregated from the general populace, it is very comforting to forget about such a nasty person

17

and revert to our own carefully constructed, private worlds. The fact that the criminal will some day be back in the community is not an immediate problem and is soon forgotten, if it is ever consciously realized at all.

Even if the vast majority of people in jail are there awaiting trial (and, therefore, presumed innocent) on relatively minor charges, there is a presumption that they are somehow "bad." Otherwise, innocent or guilty, they would never have been locked up at all. The media reinforces this belief by such indulgent (and almost exclusive) reportage of heinous crimes (such stories sell papers) and neglect of most other aspects of crime and criminal justice that the typical citizen soon comes to believe that the atypical "newsworthy" crime is, in fact, the commonplace occurrence. The abundance of highly fictional "cop shows" on television further gives the average citizen an unrealistic and often distorted view of crime and criminal justice American style.

The "out of sight, out of mind" mentality virtually ensures that there will be little effective oversight of jail operations. Furthermore, the high walls or electrified fences surrounding many facilities serve as a foreboding method of keeping the public out as well as the prisoners in. Even if a concerned citizen desired to find out, short of actual commitment, what conditions in the local jail were, the oppressive institutional appearance and maze of regulations and procedures would soon dampen the enthusiasm for inquiry. Unlike so many other public services, most especially the police, jails operate in a clandestine environment in which the public and even elected officials are almost compelled to rely on the administrator for information about operations, unless an escape or riot suddenly focuses community attention on the facility. "Out of sight, out of mind" means that almost anything can occur in the local jail and only the staff and inmates will ever know. The staff has an obvious self-interest to protect; the inmates generally come from the lowest socioeconomic groups, which have the least credibility, power, and influence to stimulate or demand remedial action.

Lack of Constitutency

Public apathy leads directly to perhaps the greatest single problem confronting jails and the entire field of corrections, i.e., the lack of an effective political constitutency. This is in direct contradistinction to virtually every other major public service provided by government. The only people who are immediately and directly affected by jail operations are inmates, and they cannot vote while incarcerated for obvious and practical reasons (although in most instances they retain their franchise).

By way of illustration, if Congress tomorrow were to suddenly pass legislation that substantially and adversely affected public assistance recipients or environmental interests or any one of hundreds of constituten-cies, within hours thousands of telegrams, phone calls, and people would descend upon the Capitol. If Congress were to similarly pass legislation worsening jail conditions, wardens and sheriffs would hardly open the front doors of their institutions to permit a massive prisoners' march on Washington. Of course, every citizen in a community is hurt in one way or another over the long term by an abominable jail. But since the harm is neither immediate nor necessarily direct, the average person does not perceive his or her self-interest to be at stake in the matter, which is a crucial element in stimulating organization and action for reform.

In the ever-escalating battle for a share of limited or dwindling public revenues, it is easy to understand how jails are relegated to last place at the appropriations table. A mayor or county executive is faced with many wor-thy and competing community needs. Is an improved jail more important to the community at large than better schools, a new public hospital, improved public transportation, etc.? The choices and alternatives are certainly not easy, no matter how objective a process was employed to render the final decisions. But when political leaders also realize that positive attention to each of these other areas means pleasing a major constituency and results therefore in votes, the outcome of the battle of the budget is assured not just for one year but for every year. It is this endemic and perpetual neglect of jail needs that contributes so substantially to the prevalence of abominable conditions. Ironically, should a major riot or similar catastrophy ever transpire, thereby compelling major attention, the costs of remediation are substantially higher than proper funding would have been initially.

No local official is ever reelected because his or her administration has given the city or county the best jail in the state. Without a viable political constituency to publicly insist upon adequate jail facilities and administra-tion, there is no pragmatic incentive for political leaders to initiate signifi-cant action. If anything, such action might even be considered a political liability, since it may well be perceived as being "soft" on crime and criminals or, at least, an inappropriate diversion of resources away from other desirable public services or community objectives.

Neglect by the Corrections Profession

If one were to conceive of the field of corrections as a much maligned, neglected, and poverty-stricken subculture, surely jails would be relegated to the lowest caste. Within corrections, whatever power, "glamour," and influence that may exist is concentrated in the state and federal penal systems. The so-called desirable or prestige jobs are those of warden or superintendent of a state prison, state commissioner of corrections, or their equivalents in the Federal Bureau of Prisons. Among workers in the field, as with the general public, it is the San Quentins and Leavenworths that are the household names, not the anonymous county jails. Even a major professional organization, the American Correctional Association, has no specific committee or other internal organizational entity devoted to jails within a structure in which formal, special, and ad hoc committees seemingly abound.[1] The hierarchy of the corrections field is so ordered that the appropriate career ladder for a competent and experienced jail staff member entails eventual "graduation" into a state prison system. The best county or city facility is considered "minor league," while even the worst state system is thought of as the "big time."

The correctional establishment finds it convenient to denigrate the role of the local detention and short-term sentenced jails. Its members correctly cite the enormity of the problem—dismal conditions, the large number of jails, the plethora of responsible jurisdictions and political authorities, and so on. Furthermore, the correctional establishment pays homage to and continually fosters the myth that jails do not have prisoners long enough to effect some sort of rehabilitation. In effect, these people are saying that corrections should wait until a petty thief, serving 90 to 180 days in jail, becomes an armed robber, serving 5 to 10 years in a penitentiary, before intervention in his criminal career should be attempted. They are also, of course, overlooking the fact, well learned in other helping social services, that it is the intensity of treatment, not the duration, that is the key element in determining eventual success. What the establishment is also not so subtly implying is that they have enough problems of their own to contend with in prisons without worrying about nearly 4000 jails.

In terms of sheer numbers, it is a far more simple matter to organize 50 state prison systems than 4000 somewhat autonomous jails. This is especially true when one recalls that most of these local institutions are administered by sheriffs, who owe primary allegiance to the law enforcement field and its organizations, not to corrections. Thus it is relatively easy to concentrate organized correctional efforts exclusively on the enhancement of state prisons and penal systems, virtually to the total exclusion of jails. Even if correctional leaders were to point out that the majority of sheriffs who oversee jails give prime allegiance to the law enforcement profession, there are still plenty of nonsheriff jail administrators with whom to establish meaningful dialogue.

The net results of this professional neglect are significant. In practical terms, the local jail administrator is made to feel like an outsider within his own profession and lacks the potential strong support that other professional groups, such as doctors and lawyers, enjoy from their national organizations. By keeping jails relegated to a distinctly second class relationship to the rest of the field, the correctional establishment is assured that its viewpoints will predominate when national commissions and study groups are established to examine the field and recommend potentially beneficial legislation and the expenditure of federal funds. This professional predominance has served to guarantee that regulations and distribution mechanisms for federal funding, such as the Law Enforcement Assistance Administration (LEAA) with a recent annual budget of more than $800 million, substantially favor the state correctional systems. Perhaps this situation would be acceptable if it could be demonstrated that the role of state prisons is a more significant one in the fight against crime, or that state systems are manifestly more qualified, by virtue of proven competence and attempted innovation, to receive and expend "manna" from Washington. Such proof, however, simply does not exist.

Thus the lack of a viable political constituency in the community is compounded by the lack of an effective voice in and support by the correctional establishment. This ensures that whatever assistance may be given to the field will be allotted to state prisons first, leaving precious little for jails. Without an effective political power base on the local level, this professional ostracism closes the doors to state and national legislative and bureaucratic recognition of the needs and problems of jails and thus to the potential additional assistance with which to deal with them.

The Role of the Sheriff

Most of this nation's jails are run by sheriffs. What are sheriffs doing in the jail business? This practice is a long-standing tradition that goes back to the somewhat primitive beginnings of a formal criminal justice system in America. In colonial times, corporal punishment, incapacitation, and public humiliation were the primary methods used to deal with the convicted criminal. Incarceration in "gaols" was used merely to ensure that the accused would be present in court on the day of trial. Concepts such as "serving time," rehabilitation, and even the separation of prisoners by age and sex had not yet been "invented." The sheriff, who at that time was *the* law enforcement official (since police departments had not been invented yet either), was given this additional chore, which was seen as related to public safety.

Times have changed. The administration of justice has become far more specialized and complex. Why, then, are sheriffs still in the jail business? There is no convincing answer, other than historical tradition. Sheriffs are elected law enforcement officials whose background, training, and interest usually lay in the area of criminal investigation and the apprehension of criminals. While in some areas sheriffs primarily have civil as opposed to criminal responsibilities, in many rural areas they are still elected as the principal policing official in the county, and their reelection hinges on how well the public perceives them to have performed that function.

In most instances, administering the jail is just an additional responsibility that comes with the job and bears little relationship to the political realities of the office. The typical sheriff has little or no training or background in jail administration and his interest and attention is directed mainly to the policing aspect of criminal justice. A sheriff's identification, therefore, is typically with law enforcement not corrections, and his effectiveness (or lack of it) in running the jail has little or no bearing on his political career.

The result is that quite often scant attention is given to management of the jail. That duty is most frequently delegated almost completely to a trusted deputy. The process of selecting jail guards (who are most often also deputy sheriffs) is highly suspect in many instances. Since the sheriff's interests and career potential usually reside in his enforcement role, the brighter, more competent deputies are naturally assigned to policing duties. Guards, therefore, are those people who have not performed adequately in their law enforcement assignments. Sometimes deputies are also assigned to the jail as a sabbatical from the rigors of law enforcement in the community. Some sheriffs also use the jail as part of their training program for new recruits. Patronage considerations significantly enter into the process of hiring jail employees in some counties, since this is one way of enhancing a political organization.

Of course, there are some notable exceptions to my rather grim depiction of sheriff-operated jails. A number of sheriffs in every section of the country have extended considerable time, talent, resources, and interest into markedly improving their local jails and trying innovative approaches to jail management and rehabilitation. Furthermore, in major metropolitan jurisdictions with sizable facilities, the responsible sheriffs often do quite creditable jobs of administration. This results from the fact that the type of sheriff elected in such areas either possesses a more sophisticated background and broader qualifications than does his rural counterpart and/or the jail has too many prisoners and too large a budget to be ignored.

Several jurisdictions have recently restructured the role of the sheriff and removed many of the law enforcement functions from the job. In such instances, the jail becomes a significant segment of the sheriff's responsibilities in terms of budget and staffing complement and thus a major component of his power base. Under such circumstances, some sheriffs have suddenly become quite interested in learning about jail administration, since a well-run, effective jail is now perceived as a political asset.

In addition to the efforts of some sheriffs on the local level, the National Sheriffs' Association, a powerful organization, has made occasional attempts to enhance jail administration by sheriffs by holding regional training workshops and obtaining federal grants to prepare and issue training manuals and handbooks. But these efforts are dependent, of course, upon the willingness of the membership to utilize these tools.

Besides the staffing problems and the frequently cavalier attitudes toward jail administration, other abuses can also occur in sheriff-operated jails. For example, until 1975, when two federal court decisions effectively ended the practice, a few counties still employed a fee system in running the local jail. Under this arrangement, the sheriff received a fixed sum of money per day from the county for each person confined in the jail. Ostensibly, these funds were to be used for the care and custody of the prisoners. But an unscrupulous sheriff could decide to make wholesale arrests of various nondangerous community outcasts, even knowing that most of them would be set free as soon as they were brought before a judge. Since the people had been admitted to the jail, the sheriff would receive the fee from the county, thereby turning a handsome and legal (though dubiously Constitutional) profit. By cutting back on the amount and quality of food served, the sheriff could also make a very nice personal "bonus" from the jail's operation.

The solution to this general problem of sheriff-run jails seems obvious. Either so restructure the job that jail management becomes the sheriff's primary, if not sole, responsibility or place jails under the authority of a professional correctional administrator. Proper jail management is too complex and too important today to be entrusted to someone whose qualifications, interests, and professional future are in another field. No jail can be efficient or effective if its employees change after every election, as is the case in a number of counties. The obvious solution, however, is not always the most feasible one. Since most jails in America are located in comparatively small jurisdictions and hold an average of less than 25 prisoners, it may well be too expensive to separate the jail function from the sheriff's office. Where, too, would one find so many qualified jail administrators to run all these jails? Furthermore, there is scant likelihood in the near future that voters in hundreds of jurisdictions will suddenly vote to amend state constitutions and/or restructure county and municipal governments to effect an administrative change that solely impacts the jail. Realistically, therefore, sheriffs will continue to run the vast majority of jails for the foreseeable future. Hence, reality dictates that significant efforts be directed toward educating and training sheriffs to become more proficient jail managers. The establishment of separate local correctional agencies to run jails does not guarantee major improvements in conditions and managerial acumen and the qualified personnel to carry out such a reorganization simply do not exist in sufficient numbers to make such a move practical at this time. By a concerted effort to work with sheriffs to effect jail reform, no doubt some degree of improvement can be accomplished. Indeed, it would be an achievement of no small dimensions if those "Support Your Local Sheriff" bumper stickers were some day to read "Support Your Local Jail".

Misuse of Jails

Far too often, jails serve as dumping grounds for society's problem children, many of whom are either not criminals or pose no real threat to public safety. Chronic alcoholics, for example, charged only with drinking their 99 cent wine in public, fill many jails, even though in several federal judicial districts such a charge has been deemed unconstitutional. The insane are often jailed, presumably pending a judicial commitment and subsequent transfer to a mental hospital—a process that may take weeks or even months. A few jurisdictions even place neglected and dependent children, whose only "crime" is that they have been subjected to hideous abuses or wanton neglect by their parents, in confinement. True, a juvenile court will eventually make a disposition of their situations and make a more suitable placement, but one can only postulate the additional harm done to these youngsters by exposing them to hard-core delinquents and criminals in an atmosphere that could hardly be called wholesome.

The point is that most of these people do not belong in jail. Their offenses are not fundamentally criminal in nature. If anything, they may be eyesores to the body politic but certainly not threats to its safety and well-being. Jails are simply neither equipped nor staffed to properly deal with the acute and specialized needs of these people, nor, in all probability, will they ever be. These individuals are medical, mental health, social, or welfare cases, needing a variety of treatments and facilities; they are *not* criminals. Apparently, as long as such people are no longer on the streets in plain view, the community assumes the problem solved, no matter the means employed to do so.

The result of this process is tragic in human terms and serves to so overburden and overcrowd the jails that there is a near total breakdown in the system. The local jail cannot devote its major energies to performing its functions of security and rehabilitation of the criminal offender when its meager resources are taxed severely in trying to provide bed space and the basic needs for its "Noah's ark" of human social problems. The aging alcoholic whose foot is gangrenous needs a hospital first and a residential alcoholism program or a rest home second. Grilled gates and cell bars do neither him nor society any good. The insane need proper mental health facilities, not hypersecure isolation—about the best that most jails can provide—which may only serve to exacerbate the problem. An eight-year-old victim of repeated beatings, who has also been used as a human ashtray, needs love and kindness, not the clanging of steel doors and the "attentions" of an aggressive, homosexual teenage delinquent. As long as these people are brought to jail via proper procedure, the administrator has no authority to turn them away. This problem lies not with jails per se, but with the communities that permit their flagrant misuse.

Overuse

In a typical American county, a mother with two children and receiving public assistance is arrested and jailed on a charge of disorderly conduct. While the woman is spending 30 days in jail, her children are temporarily housed in a county shelter. Normally, the county would pay $28.75 as its share of the assistance payment (the figures are from 1969—while the costs have escalated, the criminal justice policy has remained the same). But with the mother incarcerated, the county's expenditures rise to $131 for jail costs and another $700 to house the children—a difference in excess of $800 more than the county's public assistance obligation.[2] (These figures do not reflect the substantial, additional costs of apprehension, prosecution, judicial administration, and the like.) Upon release, of course, the mother and children are reunited.

What has the county accomplished by spending this extra $800? Nothing, except the further deterioration of that particular family's circumstances. Does being guilty of disorderly conduct create such a dire menace to the community that it is necessary to isolate the perpetrator under conditions of extreme security? Or would the county have been wiser to save the $800 outlay and spend a part of the cost-savings to provide some sort of relevant social services that would help improve the family's ability to more adequately survive in society?

Thousands of people are confined over long periods in jails while awaiting trials merely because they cannot afford to pay a $50 bondsman's fee to secure release on a bond of $500—an amount that strongly indicates that the crime involved is of a comparatively minor nature. Currently in New York City it costs $71.87 just to incarcerate one person for one night.[3] Such an expenditure does not result from trying to turn New York's jails into resort hotels for the confined—an assertion of which the city's facilities have never been guilty—but rather from salaries of guards, institution maintenance and administration, and similar costs. This is a substantial amount to expend merely to lock up a person who is in jail primarily because of his or her inability to raise a paltry sum to pay a token bail. Is this person a sufficient threat to the community to justify such an expenditure? Would the community demand a change in the system if it were aware of the amount of tax dollars involved? In this example there has not even been an attempt to indicate the effects of such practices upon the quality of justice—the inhibiting limitations imposed upon preparation of an adequate defense at the trial. The truly dangerous, successful criminal knows no such limits, since he can afford to buy freedom on virtually any bail a judge might set.

Even after sentencing, money can still have an enormous effect on the amount of time served. Many counties impose court costs on the guilty, and they must serve extra time if payment of these costs cannot be made promptly. In effect, the county is paying $20 to $30 a day in hopes of recovering an often paltry sum. A particularly egregious example of this is the story of a man in his sixties who spent a year in jail for shooting at a deer—and missing! He just could not pay the court costs and fine imposed.

You might well be wondering at this point if I am suggesting that no one should be in jail. This is decidedly not the case; rather what I am saying is that the underlying concepts of bail and jail are being perverted at tremendous costs to the community and to those involuntarily thrown into the criminal justice process. The fundamental purpose of bail is to ensure that the accused will show up for trial. Also, bail can be used as a means of temporarily isolating a presumed dangerous offender from society while that person is awaiting trial. Admittedly, this latter purpose of bail is hotly disputed as unconstitutional by some attorneys. Unlike traffic fines, bail is not a revenue producer for local government, only for bondsmen. If a person is *not* a threat to the community and has local ties that would indicate that she or he will not flee the jurisdiction prior to a trial, then being jailed for failure to raise a bondsman's fee constitutes a penalty for being poor and results in an unwarranted waste of public funds; this contravenes any rational definition of the term *justice*.

A jail exists to protect the public, in the short term, by confining dangerous people and, in the long term, by rehabilitating offenders. The prevalent fortress-like construction of jails constitutes an architecturally derived neon sign advertising its purpose. Yet so many of the "guests" of these medieval monstrosities are not dangerous, nor have they been charged with serious crimes. They are there primarily because the jail exists, and thus it is easier to overfill it than to develop alternatives for effectively dealing with these people.

In a consideration of who should or should not be in jail, ironies abound. A particularly poignant example is that in some states there are no statutory provisions for placing misdemeanants on probation, while felons are fully eligible for consideration of such disposition by the courts. In other jurisdictions, while misdemeanant probation may be authorized, probation agencies and courts make no provision to implement it, spending all of their time instead working with felons. This is not to speak against probation for felons, but surely if felons are eligible for probation, shouldn't misdemeanants also be eligible, especially when one considers that, by definition, misdemeanants are less dangerous to the community? In practice what this means is that the armed robber may serve his or her time under supervision in the community, while the petty thief (one who takes less than $100 or its equivalent) serves the entire sentence in jail.

What is needed is greater emphasis on diversion from jail incarceration. *Diversion*, in essence, is nothing more than "decisions which provide alternatives to the traditional sequence of arrest-trial-conviction-sentence-incarceration."[4] No one suggests that every offender should be diverted. Jails should still be used for people who cannot safely be allowed to remain uncontrolled in the community. Thus diversion efforts must be accompanied by thorough and effective screening techniques to ensure wise decisionmaking and afford the community the measure of public safety to which it is entitled.

Some major types of diversion are: use of citations by the police in lieu of arrest; court-authorized release on personal recognizance or in third-party custody while awaiting trial; supervised release in the community in lieu of continuing confinement; and referral or civil commitment of such special offender groups as alcoholics and drug addicts to appropriate facilities and treatment programs.[5] Certainly there are a number of jurisdictions in which one or more of these diversion techniques has been tried and failed. However, if the specifics of the failure are examined, almost inevitably the cause is improper screening and/or staff incompetence, which is not a reflection of the validity of the diversion concept but rather of the circumstances of its implementation.

As long as jails exist, there will be a communal tendency to fill them because, not unlike Mt. Everest, they are there. Such an attitude represents a wanton waste of tax dollars, gross mismanagement of public services, and, in many cases, a denial of the fundamental tenets of the American system of justice. No one is advocating that people who are in fact a threat to public safety should be allowed to avoid confinement. But there are many jail inmates who do not fall into this category. There are less-expensive, more-equitable, and more-effective ways to deal with these people that will convey substantial cost benefits to the communities and badly needed services to the individuals directly involved. A proper utilization of diversion techniques would also enable jails to concentrate on achieving their objectives with the truly criminal offenders and relieve several major operational problems, not the least of which is overcrowding. Humane considerations aside, such an approach constitutes the only rational approach to management of existing criminal justice and related public resources. In an age of civil penury, it is absurd to continue to "spend $50,000 on a $50 case."[6] When the results of traditional approaches are considered in human terms, their perpetuation is inexcuseable in a civilized society.

Lack of Personnel Standards and Training

From what has been stated thus far, it is obvious that jails suffer from a paucity of appropriate rehabilitation specialists, an inadequate number of guards in many cases, and largely unqualified administrators. Part of this personnel problem has external causes, i.e., low salaries and abominable public image. Some communities pay their zoo keepers more than they pay those who care for confined human beings. Just as in virtually every other field of endeavor, one gets what one pays for.

This pay problem is exacerbated by the low esteem in which corrections work is held as a career. Rare indeed is the household in which little Johnny enthusiastically announces, "When I grow up, I want to be a warden." If he did, a hurried visit to the school psychologist would probably ensue. By a more formal means of measurement, a Louis Harris poll showed that a corrections career was deemed least desirable as a vocational choice by high school students.[7] The combination of low salary scales and low societal esteem has a significantly detrimental effect on efforts to recruit the types of talented personnel who are most urgently needed in the jail field.

There are currently no mandatory minimum qualifications imposed by either the states or federal government for jail personnel. In most areas the job applicant must be at least 21 years old, have one or two years of prior work experience (at what, is apparently immaterial), and be of "good moral character," a phrase that is rarely defined. Some jails require that employees also be high school graduates or the equivalent. There are no specific skills or talents mandated, and the screening of applicants could hardly be considered either refined or sophisticated. Several states have established commissions or study groups to develop recommended minimum qualifications. Presumably, if the standards are fully developed, these states will eventually compel compliance as a condition for receiving various types of state assistance.

Training would seem to be an absolute necessity in view of the lack of hiring standards and qualifications. Unfortunately, with few exceptions, training is haphazard at best. In most jails, training might well be categorized as "good luck" on-the-job training. The new guard reporting for duty is given a uniform and a set of keys, is wished "good luck," and is put to work. In such a situation, the new employee will most likely not want to continually bother supervisors with petty operational questions; and since there is no one else to ask, the inmates break him or her in via an informal conditioning program designed to ensure a happy home on the cellblock. Some jails will assign a new recruit to work with an experienced guard for a short time as a more formal version of on-the-job training. The drawback to this approach is that unless the experienced employee has received some training, he or she is likely to impart numerous bad habits and erroneous procedures to the trainee, thus perpetuating the basic problem.

Where there is a commitment to an intelligently designed and implemented staff training effort, many, though not all, shortcomings of the personnel system can be surmounted. By combining internal resources with those of the community (community colleges, for example, in which training for guards is largely paid for by federal funds), a certain minimal level of competence can be attained. But, like all other improvements in the jail field, the development of sound and ongoing training requires ingenuity and energetic work on the part of administration. Since jails operate 24 hours a day, 365 days a year, even an exceptional warden cannot achieve a total reformation of a bad institution alone. Staff development and training is a key element in making a jail a truly "correctional" facility. It is the current lack of staff depth in almost all correctional settings that has ensured that rehabilitative concepts have never been given a fair test and accounts for many of the security oversights that result in escapes or serious injuries to both personnel and inmates.

Lack of an Orderly Release System

Typically, on the day of release from jail, individuals are given back their "street" clothes and whatever other personal property they had with them at the time of commitment; then they are abruptly ushered through the exit back into the free world. What is happening, in effect, is that the person is suddenly thrust back into the community without any assistance in making a readjustment to a social environment in which he or she previously has experienced obvious and substantial difficulty.

In so many instances, the releasees are in a far worse position to "make it" than they were before incarceration. If he or she had a job, it has been lost; if the family unit is still in tact, relationships have no doubt been strained; finances have suffered; the car, furniture, and so on may well have been repossessed; and housing and employment must now be secured, although ex-offenders have probably lost whatever positive community contacts they may have had prior to incarceration and have little or no money to tide them over until their first pay checks. In many ways, incarceration virtually constitutes economic execution. Yet the worst, most lasting effect of a jail term is the resulting stigma, which adds to the already formidable difficulty of obtaining employment and other similar necessities. It is little wonder that the criminal justice system is sometimes referred to as a revolving door, i.e., arrest, conviction, incarceration, rearrest, reincarceration.

What is needed is an orderly release system that takes into account the problems the inmate will encounter upon return to society. Some measures must be established that will prepare the individual for successful reacculturation to the community and assist in the initial (and most difficult) stages of that reintegration. No doubt other measures could also be devised that could coordinate criminal justice and community efforts. In cases in which no public threat is involved, virtually all inmates should be given a chance to participate in work or training release programs. With work release, the inmate would hold a job in the community during the day and return to the institution at night. Thus he or she would be accruing savings, contributing to the support and maintenance of his or her family, have a job to go to upon release, and become used to life in the realistic conditions of the free world on a graduated basis. Training release, whereby the inmate participates in vocational training in the community and returns to the jail at night, would provide a usable job skill upon release and reacculturation benefits similar to those of work release. This reacculturation process would certainly reduce the shocks that normally accompany release.

A number of counties have a statutory provision, which is rarely used, to establish a system of jail parole. This release system entails a board that determines if the inmate no longer poses a threat to society and has merited release. Upon release and for the remaining portion of the original sentence, the person would be supervised by a parole or probation officer. In addition to ensuring compliance with the terms of release, this officer would also help the individual in finding housing and employment, provide or obtain appropriate counseling and/or other social services, and in general serve as a constructive resource in the community to whom the former prisoner could turn for advice and assistance. Such a system would surely further the ends of both public safety and lasting rehabilitation of the offender far more than the current "here's your stuff and there's the door" approach.

Even the establishment of some sort of inhouse prerelease needs assessment and planning by jail staff would be a marked improvement over current nonprocedures and practices. If coordinated with interested community assistance groups, such as the Salvation Army, Jaycees, and so on, and appropriate governmental agencies, like the state employment service, such jail prerelease programs could provide significant assistance to inmates in their struggle to "make it" upon the termination of their sentences.

The current release nonsystem ensures a high percentage of failure among ex-inmates. Expanded work or training release participation, county parole, and/or establishment of coordinated prerelease programs are just a few of the more obvious improvements that could be made now to reduce the traffic through the revolving door; and the cost would be minimal.

Conclusions

The foregoing discussion of components of the jail problem is by no means a comprehensive inventory. Sentencing procedures, archaic statutes, the fiscal and budgetary processes, as well as many other aspects of jail and correctional operations could and should also be carefully examined. And these constitute the mere micro aspects of the problem. A complete listing should also include factors relating to the schools, employment markets, racism, and many other areas of social difficulty and public service delivery that impact upon crime and its correction. But just concentrating on those facets of the problem examined in this chapter should be sufficient to indicate that while there are many problems that can and should be solved within the jail itself and the larger criminal justice system, jails are a community institution and solutions must be developed and implemented in, with, and by the specific community if they are to be at all effective or permanent.

So many factors that significantly impact the daily operation of the jail are wholly beyond the influence and authority of the jail administrator to alter. In functioning as his "brother's keeper," the jailer is in some ways confined by the community at large within the constraints of a larger system of governmental and political influences over which he has little control and upon which he is almost wholly dependent for the tools with which to do his or her job. The hope for more effective jails lies not with bigger walls and tougher steel, but in a concerted effort for community understanding and support of an often disconcerting and neglected but necessary and important institution. Ultimately, it is in every community's self-interest to develop this effort.

3

Security

You can't treat 'em, if you don't have 'em.

Old Penological Maxim

Purposes

Security (custody) in a jail relates to those methods and procedures invoked to maintain order within the institution and to prevent escapes. It is, therefore, primarily concerned with one of the major objectives of corrections, i.e., protection of the public. In a correctional setting such matters as prisoner supervision and transportation, property control, and control of contraband (weapons, narcotics, alcohol, etc.), are considered to fall under the mantle of security.

A major function of security is to ensure the physical safety of both inmates and staff. Unless this is successfully accomplished, rehabilitation efforts within the jail are meaningless. If an inmate is justifiably in constant fear of assault or worse, survival, not concentration on self-improvement programs, will naturally be his or her overriding concern. Unfortunately, as reports emanating from numerous jails now indicate, this functional objective is by no means universally achieved for whatever reasons. Safe jails are mandatory, if they are ever to hope to contribute to assuring safe streets.

Organization and Management

In the real world of jail administration, security is given marked priority over rehabilitation. While the two are often mentioned in the same breath, there is little question that security is the first among equals. In most institutions virtually all other activities and functions are subordinated to security. The reason for this is quite simple, i.e., no jail administrator has ever been fired for failing to rehabilitate an inmate, while many have been dismissed following escapes or disturbances.

There is certainly nothing wrong with putting safety first. But when security becomes such a predominant concern to the virtual exclusion of all other aspects of jail operation, the facility is more of a human warehouse than a *correctional* institution. This predominance has served to stifle pro-

33

gram innovation and has perpetuated traditional management models, since no one can be blamed for following the "book," no matter how outdated it may be. Consequently, from the perspective of intrainstitutional politics, security will invariably win out; and both staff and inmates know this. The tragic irony is that for all the emphasis on security, jails are still not safe.

By far the largest category of employees in any jail is that of guard or correctional officer. These are the people who supervise the prisoners, guard the gates, and perform other duties pertaining to overall institutional security. They are organized in a quasi-military chain of command, i.e., guard, sergeant, lieutenant, and, in the very large jails, captain and major. In medium-sized and large jails, there is usually a deputy warden for security, who is responsible for the administration of the custody function. In the small jails, this function is usually carried out directly by the warden or chief jailer.

It should be noted, however, that all employees have a security responsibility, but that duty is primary for the custody staff. A teacher, for example, is essentially employed in a rehabilitation capacity, but still must observe the general rules established for institutional security and, if at all possible, prevent any serious incident from occurring by proper cooperation with his or her counterparts in security. If the teacher is told, for instance, by a "student" that somebody in the next cell has a knife and is going to stick it into the sergeant, there is a fundamental obligation to transmit this information.

On an operational basis, it must be remembered that jails function 24 hours per day, 365 days per year. Hence, the guards are assigned to work on one of three eight-hour tours of duty. Regular assignment to longer work hours has the effect of significantly reducing the alertness and powers of observation of the officer.

Any part of the jail that requires the presence of a guard for all or part of a shift is known as a *post*. Obviously, since there is continuous traffic in and out of jails, the front gate or main entrance would be a 24-hour post, i.e., it requires a full-time guard on each shift. By contrast, the recreation yard would need only an officer(s) during the time it is in use. As a general principle, an officer(s) should be physically present in housing units whenever there are inmates present. Some variation on this standard may be permissible when other means of effecting continual supervision are utilized, e.g., television cameras. It is amazing, but in some jails that are sufficiently staffed to provide continuous cellblock supervision, this principle is not carried out. The lack of such supervision can and does often result in assaults, escape attempts, and the introduction of contraband. It is also axiomatic that there should be a guard assigned to any activity or part of the jail where a number of inmates are gathered. Under no circumstances, should inmates be allowed to supervise or have any authority over other inmates.

Since a jail operates around the clock seven days per week and guards are performing a variety of tasks and functions in many disparate parts of the facility, it is impossible for a jail administrator to be able to personally provide a fitting degree of employee supervision. Each shift in a medium or large facility does, of course, have a uniformed officer (sergeant, lieutenant, or captain) in charge, but this person does not make policy or procedure, merely seeing that such policy is implemented. With three shifts of employees actually operating the jail, it is not at all unusual to find that because of a managerial failure to properly and effectively communicate policies and procedures, each shift does its "own thing" to some degree or implementation of policy is based upon the shift supervisor's best recollection of what "I think they wanted in this type of situation." On the day shift, this is not such a crucial problem, since administrators are present in the jail during these hours and are thus available for query. But on the other two shifts, the lack of clear policies and procedures results all too frequently in confusion, inconsistency, and, in a number of instances, serious incidents. If, for example, an officer or shift supervisor is not sure what to do when an inmate is threatened by another inmate and must delay action for undue deliberation or to find out what is the proper procedure, a stabbing or some similar untoward event might well result.

To ensure the proper degree of communication and the operational benefits and efficiencies accruing therefrom, it is essential for jail administrators to clearly enunciate and disseminate all policies and procedures. The first step in this process is the compilation and issuance to all staff members of a manual that contains such material. For convenience in updating and revising this information, it is advisable for the manual to be prepared in looseleaf form in a binder so that outdated documents can be readily discarded and replaced. This ensures that all staff have direct access to the information that should guide the daily operation of the facility.

Another essential means of providing appropriate managerial direction in the actual day-to-day functioning of the jail is the preparation of a comprehensive set of post orders for each security post in the jail. "Post orders tell an employee on a particular job . . . what he is supposed to do and when. Post orders are especially important in those jobs covered by jail officers, since these employees rotate from job to job and shift to shift. Post orders are essential to controlling jail activities since an officer can cover a post he has never worked before after a few minutes of reading and do it efficiently."[1] Much of the information in the post orders relates to tasks that must be performed at specific times in order to maintain the institution's schedule, e.g., "Noon: take inmates to day room for lunch." These orders, therefore, should clearly indicate which tasks are mandatory at which times and which are discretionary for the officer. But with a current and complete set of post orders to which to refer, the officer should be able to efficiently carry out his or her duties in a manner consistent with overall jail policies and procedures.

Yet another vehicle for reviewing and disseminating relevant information to staff members is the staff meeting. These should be held on a regularly scheduled basis. Staff meetings also can serve as an appropriate forum for the administration to receive feedback from supervisory and line employees on the practical impact and effects of existing operational methodologies and to encourage input into any contemplated changes in existing practices from the people who will be responsible for their actual implementation.

Both initial (preservice) and ongoing (inservice) training efforts also provide an opportunity for policy and procedural dissemination and review.

Even with all proper managerial guidelines and frames of reference in place, it is still incumbent upon jail administrators to get out and see for themselves what is going on in their facilities. It is also essential to maintain constant communication with shift supervisory personnel both to ensure their thorough understanding of the spirit as well as the letter of written guidelines and to maintain continuing contact with the day-to-day operations of the jail. Supervisory security personnel are in many ways the key to effective custody and smooth operations, since they are the link between management and line staff. Again, since jails are a 24-hour-per-day operation, it is the supervisory level of staff that provides the continuity and on-the-spot direction upon which, to a large degree, the entire efficiency of the institution is based. A warden cannot run the jail alone—it takes coordination and the competence of the supervisory employees to create the stability needed for other staff to function effectively.

Predisposing Factors to Good Security

A jail is a microsociety which, like any other society, is a sum of interpersonal interactions, internal factors, and external influences. Hence, in establishing and maintaining a sound program of security, it is naive to assume that a sufficient number of well-trained officers *alone* will assure safety within the facility and prevent most escapes. Not unlike its free world societal counterpart, there are a number of conditions which, if present, can lead to a substantial escalation in tensions or exacerbate existing inadequacies to the point of explosion. Some of these conditions in a jail, e.g., severe overcrowding, may be beyond the direct control of the administrator. However, even then, overcrowding by itself without added impetus from other factors never caused a riot, although it may well have served to add to or exaggerate preexisting failures within the jail's operation.

In general, there are a number of factors which, if successfully addressed, can serve to keep frustrations and tensions at a low level, thus reinforcing security. It must be remembered that virtually any activity in a jail has an effect upon all other parts of the facility's operation. Some of the factors that can serve to create an atmosphere that can significantly reduce or prevent security problems are:

Good communication between staff and inmates

"Empathy or understanding on the part of staff—ability to anticipate the inmate's responses, to walk in his shoes, to understand his personality"[2] and problems

Clean, bright housing units, which, if at all possible, permit some privacy for the inmates

Good food that is ample in quantity, quality, and palatability

Equal and fair enforcement of rules and regulations

Provision of an adequate channel by which inmates may present and seek redress of grievances

A sound classification system

Good medical care

Provision for frequent visiting by family and friends

Odd as the idea may at first seem to some people, sound and adequate programming can well be the best security measure a jail can implement. As the American Correctional Association has noted,

Perhaps, in the final analysis, the soundest and safest security measure of all *is the existence of a positive program of inmate activities.* Such a program includes all the things such as work, recreation, and education. . . . Such multifaceted programs are sometimes referred to as "calculated risks" against security. Actually, these positive programs have become important security factors in well-managed institutions of all types and have become primary security features in many institutions. . . . Prisoners who are receiving decent food and humane treatment and who are busily engaged in useful work programs, carefully organized and purposeful leisure time activities, and self-improvement, seldom resort to disturbances or escape attempts. No matter how modern the buildings, how secure the facilities, how efficient the operating procedures may be, or how well the personnel may be trained, it should be emphasized that security cannot be assured if it is predicated entirely on procedures which are operated wholly against the will of the prisoners. If the prisoners are committed to inactivity, moral degradation, humiliation and mental stultification, then the desire within them to escape or to throw off the shackles of these unnatural restraints will become so strong that security facilities and procedures will be breached sooner or later.[3]

Like so many segments of American society, the past decade has witnessed a noticeable difference in the attitudes of people in confinement. They have become more aware of their rights and are no longer willing to remain passive and unquestioning recipients of whatever actions or inactions administrators choose to take. Recognition of this established trend reinforces the need for effective staff/inmate communication and the establishment of appropriate mechanisms for the resolution of grievances.

Prompt and positive handling of inmates' complaints and grievances is essential in maintaining good morale. A firm "no" answer can be as effective as granting his request in reducing an individual inmate's tension, particularly if he feels the problems have been given genuine consideration by appropriate officials and if given a reason for the denial. Equivocation and vague answers create false hopes and thus increase the man's anger when nothing can be done. A most dangerous situation arises, however, when inmates have grievances they feel can be corrected if only the proper officials are made aware of their problems. Inmates know that disturbances are certain if their complaints are given wide publicity when less drastic measures fail.[4]

Communication, fairness, access, and sound programming all have a major role in establishing and reinforcing a climate conducive to effective security. Guards, locks, and all the other tools of custody have a primary impact of constraining and, to some degree, preventing serious breaches of security. The best approach to security, however, is obviously one of an integrated strategy of various correctional techniques, programs, and procedures, of which custody is but one part.

Standard Security Techniques

There are a number of commonplace techniques and procedures utilized by jails throughout the nation in their security programs. This section will briefly describe a number of the more standard security techniques, i.e., counts, shakedowns, tool control, key control, cutlery control, narcotics control, and the custody implications of visiting.

Counts

Counts are a seemingly indisposable "method of knowing that the ever-present and all compelling responsibility imposed for detention of prisoners is being carried out."[5] During a count, all institutional activities come to a temporary halt and all inmates are counted. Hopefully, the total thus arrived at will equal the number of people who are supposed to be in confinement. If it does not, at least one recount is taken, attempts are made to establish the identity of the missing inmate(s), and, if the count is still "short," escape procedures are implemented. In the event of an escape, the count at least provides knowledge of a time frame within which the person(s) disappeared as an aid to investigation and apprehension.

Counts are normally taken at the three changes in shift that occur daily. In this way, responsibility for custody is transmitted from the off-going shift to the on-coming one. Many jails also have formal counts at noon. It is advisable to take an additional count sometime on the midnight shift, with the officer "checking for skin" in order to avoid the old dummy-in-the-bed trick. Hence "the count system . . . should provide for at least four official counts in a twenty-four hour period."[6] Of course, it is strongly recommended that individual officers charged with responsibility for supervising inmates make a number of informal counts during their tours of duty. This latter procedure can be done quite unobtrusively without the necessity for ceasing activity. But a cellblock officer, for example, should know at all times how many inmates are actually on the block, as well as how many, the identity, and the whereabouts of those who are not.

Shakedowns

A *shakedown* is a thorough search of a jail or any part thereof for contraband (anything an inmate has illicitly, i.e., in violation of institution rules and regulations. The definition of contraband may vary from jail to jail—weapons, alcohol, and narcotics not prescribed or approved by the jail physician are universally prohibited). All jails should be thoroughly shaken down at least once or twice per month. In addition, individual officers should be required to shake down a part of their area of responsibility each day. As a matter of fairness and decency, when a cell is shaken down, it should be left in the manner in which it was found. Leaving a cell torn up or in total disarray accomplishes no useful purpose, is a definite means of harassment, and causes understandable resentment on the part of inmates.

Frisks

Frisks are individual "pat searches" of inmates in which an officer runs his hands along the outside of an inmate's clothing to detect any contraband items of bulk that may be concealed within. The frequency of such frisks depends upon the security classification of the inmate and the area(s) to and from which he or she is coming or going. For example, if a maximum security prisoner is going from an area in which there are usually a number of tools, i.e., potential weapons, a frisk would be an appropriate, if not a mandatory, security procedure. A number of jails utilize metal detectors for this purpose instead of, or in addition to, the standard frisking technique.

Tool Control

Tool control is essential in a well-run jail, since tools can and often are used as weapons or as a means of effecting escape. Proper tool control assumes a comprehensive and continually updated inventory. All tools should be stored in secure places and be fully accounted for at the end of each work day. If tools are missing, appropriate steps should be taken immediately to recover them.

Perhaps the best method of assuring adequate tool control in an institution is the use of a "shadow board." "These are boards on which the tools are stored with the outline of the tool painted on the board so that the tool crib operator can tell at the end of the day what tools are missing."[7] When tools are checked out, a receipt or chit should be obtained and placed on the board in the place of the tool itself as an ongoing means of ensuring accountability.

Key Control

Key control is another essential element of jail security. For rather obvious reasons, inmates should never be allowed to possess or use institution keys. Extremely accurate logs and records must be kept of the existence and location of all keys, as well as to whom specific keys have been issued. Most officers, while on duty, will require the use of a number of different keys, and these are usually issued on a key ring at the beginning of each shift. As with tools, all keys must be accounted for at the end of each shift. If a missing key cannot be located promptly, there is no alternative to changing the locks affected—a costly and highly inconvenient procedure. Even if a key has been missing for only a short time, an inmate could easily have made an impression or drawing of it from which to fabricate a working copy. A number of jails utilize chit or receipt systems when issuing key rings and individual keys to employees. No key should ever be issued without an accurate record made of when and to whom it was issued, with similar documentation made of its return.

Cutlery Control

Cutlery control refers to establishing a system of accountability for all eating utensils used in the jail. Normally, kitchen equipment, such as butcher knives and other actual or potentially dangerous items, are included in the institution's tool control program. But special measures must be instituted to ensure that the cutlery used at meals is not "borrowed" and used for nefarious purposes. While a table knife is an obvious weapon, a spoon that has been sharpened at one end or a fork can be equally dangerous.

When inmates eat in communal dining halls, there is a rather standard procedure for attaining good cutlery control. This, of course, assumes that the jail maintains an accurate inventory of its silverware. When the inmates proceed into the dining room, they are each handed the appropriate eating utensils for that meal. At the end of the meal, as the inmates leave via a main exit, they must deposit the same number and type of utensils as they were initially issued into a large receptacle under the observation of an officer. If an inmate fails to do this, he is detained in the dining hall. After all inmates have left, presuming that each deposited his used cutlery as required, all the silverware is again counted before being taken back into the kitchen for washing. If any cutlery is missing, a search or shakedown should follow to recover the missing items.

When inmates eat in their cells, as is the common practice in many jails, again an officer should carefuly supervise the dispensation and return of silverware. If anything is missing, a search of the area involved should be begun promptly. The silverware should again be counted after it is returned to the institution's kitchen, since there is the possibility that trustees or other inmates may have pilfered one or more items during the course of transit from the housing units to the kitchen.

An obvious query is: Since silverware can be a cause of major security problems, why not use plastic utensils? The answer is that such plastic items are difficult to clean properly, given the equipment of most jail kitchens, and replacement after each meal would be extremely expensive and inconvenient.

Narcotics Control

Narcotics control has become a major problem in many jails, particularly those in metropolitan areas, because of the high number of addicts being confined on criminal charges. This creates an immediate and substantial demand for illicit drugs. Again, good control procedures commence with an accurate and up-to-date inventory. All narcotics should be stored under extremely secure conditions in an area removed from ready access by inmates. Dosages of medication prescribed for inmates should be prepared by qualified medical personnel, not by officers. In most jails, medication is dispensed in the cellblock areas, since there would be too many problems involved in the movement of prisoners to and from an infirmary or similar area several times a day. Medication should be dispensed personally by an officer, and the inmate should be required to swallow it in the presence of that officer. The guard should check under the tongue to ensure that indeed the medicine has been consumed and not "saved" for purposes of hoarding or sale within the institution.

Visiting

The security implications of visiting are many and varied and depend, to a large extent, upon the type of visiting procedures and facilities utilized by the jail. Any time there is a substantial number of people from the "outside" coming into and going from the jail, a threat of varying degree exists to the security of the institution—especially, today, with the smuggling of narcotics into the jail. Yet visiting is such an important activity in terms of inmate morale and the maintenance of family ties and other positive community contacts that its frequency is to be encouraged.

A number of visiting modes are used by various jails throughout the country. One common mode is the enclosed booth with a plexiglass or bullet-proof glass front in which the inmates sit while communicating with their visitors via voice-powered telephone. Some jails also use a less-structured arrangement, with inmates sitting across tables (with or without a screen in the middle) from their visitors. A third mode is a very informal, quasi-living room setting, which features sofas, easy chairs, and coffee tables in which there are few, if any, physical barriers.

Visitors, like anyone else, can easily be intimidated by oppressive security measures and are more likely to come often if the setting in which the visiting takes place is somewhat relaxed and normal. A less rigid atmosphere also encourages more open and freer communication. This is why a number of jails have tried to provide alternative settings for visiting.

Another type of visit, which is currently the source of controversy in several jurisdictions, is the "contact" visit, in which the inmate and his wife, for example, are permitted to kiss hello and good-bye and hold hands during the visit itself. Again, the purpose of this approach is to normalize the visiting as much as possible within the limits of common sense and good taste.

One key to maintaining proper security during visits is the careful screening of inmates. Obviously, a maximum security prisoner who poses an imminent escape risk or is otherwise considered dangerous should visit in the booth arrangement. The less the inmate's perceived threat to security, the less stringent the physical means of security need be. A minimum security individual who has demonstrated his or her trustworthiness could be accorded the opportunity to visit in a more relaxed atmosphere. However, under any visiting format, officers should be present and unobtrusively alert to any sign of potential trouble or attempt to pass contraband. To further ensure security, many jails frisk inmates before they are returned to their housing or work areas, and some perform a complete strip search of each inmate.

Properly structured, the provision of alternative visiting arrangements within a jail can provide a meaningful incentive for inmates. In a microsociety predicated on "don'ts," visiting alternatives give one of the few opportunities for building positive rewards into the program structure. As an inmate proves him or herself trustworthy and achieves behavioral and programmatic goals, accompanying improvement in visiting arrangements reinforces this progress and in a very important way for the inmate, since it affects his family and increases the likelihood and pleasantness of future visits. The inmate now has a very definite reason to maintain or improve upon the level of progress he or she has achieved.

However, it is also recognized that every effort made to normalize visiting arrangements also increases the risk of contraband coming into the jail. This is one of the tradeoffs in jail management—a reasonable risk is taken to achieve a desirable goal. Proper screening, alert officers, and frisks or strip searches substantially reduce the security risks involved.

Mechanical Means of Security

Yet another way of attempting to assure security is the use of various mechanical devices—fences, locks, television cameras, etc. Walls and fences are used to pose barriers to escape, which are as much psychological as practical. The use of walls has greatly declined in recent years because of the prohibitive expense involved in building them. Locks are another practical means of aiding security by preventing uncontrolled prisoner movement and denying access to certain proscribed areas. Steel grills or gates also serve the function of controlling prisoner movement, which is a key element in institutional security.

Some of the newer jails, however, have begun to replace the traditional stark cell with its frontal steel bar door with secure rooms with unbreakable windows on the doors to permit ready visibility by officers. Even though the fixtures within these rooms may still be made of unbreakable materials, this type of construction permits the inmate a semblance of privacy and reduces the oppressive psychological impact of the traditional cellular confinement. The cell, however, is still the most frequent unit of housing in jails across the country and remains so in the majority of new construction.

There is some debate currently about the extent to which television should be used for security purposes within a jail. Certainly, closed circuit units, equipped with special protection for their lenses, are often sufficient to ensure the control of various corridor gates and grills within an institution. Television monitoring in combination with speaker systems and electronic locks permit one officer in a control center to effectively supervise many such passages. Hence, the cameras are used to cover "posts," thereby reducing the number of officers who must be used for such purposes. This lowers personnel costs, so that in a short period of time the cameras pay for themselves, or at least frees up a number of guards for assignment to other functions and posts within the facility. Similar use can often be made of cameras for the main entrance and exits of the institution.

Several jails have installed small cameras on overhead tracks to supervise inmates in cellblocks. An officer outside the actual cellblock tiers or walkways monitors the pictures for signs of trouble. One problem with this approach is that while an officer might spot trouble, the response time is substantially lengthened for the officer to get to the actual scene of the problem.

Furthermore, in an overly mechanized jail, officers tend to rely on the devices exclusively, often falling into sloppy security patterns themselves in the belief that gadgetry makes the institution's security system impregnable. Inmates have frequently developed ingenious methods of overcoming even the most sophisticated equipment. Perhaps the best approach is the continual reliance on officers to provide a high degree of personal supervision of inmates with some backup supervision available via television and a greater reliance on cameras to monitor those areas in which constant personal surveillance is not warranted.

There is one operational aspect, however, in which small, mobile cameras capable of being mounted on tripods or similar contrivances have proved to be quite valuable, i.e., providing continual monitoring of suicide risks. Even if a known suicide risk is placed in a small cellblock with a high officer/inmate supervision ratio, there is no way in which a guard(s) can provide monitoring of every move. In such an instance, a small camera placed outside the cell can provide a greater degree of supervision and be a definite aid in suicide prevention.

In normal operations, one of the biggest aids to good security is communication and interaction between staff and inmates. Constant contact enables experienced and sensitive staff members to perceive problems in their incipient stages before they become crises, and allows them to perform an invaluable problem-solving role, which serves to reduce levels of tension within an institution. The overly mechanized jail, in which supervision is accomplished either extensively or exclusively by television, negates this vital function of a skilled officer and creates an impersonal atmosphere that breeds trouble. While television and other mechanical aids to security have their place in a jail, for the foreseeable future, the human element, as represented by the officers, should have the largest role in providing supervision of inmates and their activities.

Firearms

Firearms should not be permitted inside the main area of a jail except in extraordinary circumstances and with rigid controls and supervision in accordance with clearly delineated policies. The dangers of accidental discharge or of inmates "relieving" an officer of his weapon are too grievous to risk. Every jail, however, should have an arsenal, with an employee specifically designated for the proper inventory, maintenance, and servicing of weapons; and that arsenal should be kept in a most secure area, far removed from inmate access. Furthermore, jail officers should be regularly trained and qualified in the use of whatever weapons are contained in the arsenal. The use of weapons in a jail should be a last resort and the subject of much consideration prior to their use.

Emergency Plans and Procedures

Every jail should have current emergency plans and procedures in the event of fire, natural disaster, escape, or riot. These plans should be coordinated with other appropriate law enforcement, public safety, and civil defense agencies. Staff should be thoroughly trained in the implementation of these procedures and given periodic refresher training as well.

Inspection of Physical Plant

All parts of a jail should be regularly inspected from both security and safety points of view. Jails should meet all applicable fire, sanitation, and electrical codes and be kept in a clean and sanitary condition. Security apparati, including cell bars, locks, etc., should be checked frequently to ensure that they have not been tampered with and are in proper working order.

Conclusions

Obviously this one chapter cannot contain a comprehensive catalogue or discussion of all the elements, policies, and procedures involved in maintaining proper security in jails. However, the major techniques and considerations have been highlighted. In essence, it takes proper training, constant vigilance, communication, and a large application of common sense by all staff within a framework of meaningful programmatic activities to ensure the maintenance of proper order within an institution. While there is a certain element of danger inherent in any jail, this can either be heightened or reduced by organization, management, positive attitudes of staff, or lack thereof. The best designed physical plant and the most sophisticated equipment are only as effective as the people who utilize them. It is the human element that is the basis for a good security system within a jail or, if untrained and disorganized, that can lead to chaos.

4 Classification

The alternative to classification is the continuation of the "guess and by golly" system which plagued prison operation through history.
Manual of Correctional Standards

Definition and Purposes

Classification is "the separation of offenders by a variety of criteria."[1] On its most elementary level, the criteria used would be extremely obvious ones, such as sex, age (juvenile vis-à-vis adults), and legal status (sentenced or unsentenced). But since classification is also the key tool in determining inmates' custody status, which in large part dictates their housing and work assignments and matches prisoners to rehabilitation programs within the jail, there is a decided need to develop and implement sophisticated criteria appropriate for more specific classification needs. Such classification assumes the ability both to obtain sufficient information about the individual inmate and to analyze it properly.

If a jail's classification process is both efficient and accurate, security is markedly assisted and the rehabilitation program enhanced. By correctly designating prisoners as maximum, medium, or minimum security risks, custody staff is forewarned and can take the appropriate steps to ensure the maintenance of order within the institution and prevent escapes. Proper classification can do much to prevent the assaults, homosexual attacks, and other acts of violence that plague many jails. Similarly, by sagely assessing an inmate's problems and needs and matching that person to the proper program, appropriate and efficient utilization is made of the jail's rehabilitational resources.

History

To judge from the fact that 79 jails still do not separate juveniles from adults for housing purposes and more than half of America's local correctional institutions mix sentenced and unsentenced prisoners indiscriminately,[2] one might think that classification is a relatively new technique that has not become widely known or recognized in the correctional universe. In reality, Plato advocated a sophisticated concept of classification almost four hundred years before the birth of Christ.[3] As early as 1519, Spain began to separate men and women in its jails.[4] The separation of wayward boys from adults can be traced to 1650, when Filippo Franci opened a workhouse for their care and training.[5] Pope Clement XI also started a papal prison for delinquent boys in 1704 and another for women in 1735.[6]

In America, the early colonial jails or "gaols" consisted of large congregate rooms that held old and young, men and women alike. The "gaol" in the colonial Williamsburg restoration provides an example of this early mode of confinement that can be seen today. In 1790 the Walnut Street Jail in Philadelphia was converted into what would now be recognizable as a correctional facility. A key element in that conversion was the establishment of a classification system. A story from those times, which is possibly apocryphal, indicates that shortly after the separation of men and women became standard practice, the number of women confined in the Walnut Street Jail drastically declined from 40 to 4. Once established, classification to some degree became an integral part of prison administration, yet its adoption by jails in all but its most rudimentary forms has been slow.

Classification by Other Criminal Justice Agencies

Ironically, the police have always made extensive use of classification, at least on an informal basis. When an officer is called "to 'do something' about a noisy crowd of teenagers on a street corner . . . [and] decides to give them a stern warning, or a little friendly counseling in lieu of making an arrest, the officer" is making a classification decision. He has determined, based on the information provided, his or her observations at the scene, and past experience "that the youths are more annoying than dangerous, and consequently that formal arrest and intake into the criminal justice process is unwarranted."[7] In a very real sense, every sentence given by a judge is a classification decision. It remains for jails to more fully utilize and refine a technique that is rather common in the other parts of the criminal justice system.

Attitudes Toward Classification

Unfortunately, many jail administrators still do not perceive the importance of classification in the daily functioning of their operations except as a prognosticator of behavior as it affects security. Classification is somehow viewed as an unwelcome appendage to staff duties. Many administrators, for example, take a direct hand in recreation programs or other jail activities, but their attitudes toward classification seem to be "As long as I've got my chief guard on the committee, it can't do me much harm." For their own job security, these managers are concerned primarily with security and "keeping the lid on"—to the extent that classification can assist in achieving this goal, it is welcomed. But in too many instances, classification (and the honest diagnosis that is part of it) is viewed seemingly as a threat to a comforting status quo instead of as a tool for achieving *both* the ultimate goals of corrections, i.e., public safety and rehabilitation of the offender.

Organization of Classification

Depending on the size of the jail, the classification process can be implemented either through a committee or by an employee acting as a full- or part-time classification officer. In a jail with an active classification system, a newly committed inmate is usually assigned temporarily to a housing unit on the basis of age, sex, legal status, and, in some cases, the size of the bond and/or the charge. As soon as is feasible, the prisoner is interviewed by the classification officer or the classification committee for the purposes of assignment to a more permanent security status, housing unit, work activity, and program involvement. Depending on the number of newly committed inmates, this interview may take place within a day or within a week to 10 days after confinement. Of course, if the time of commitment is in the evening or on a weekend, additional days may be added to the process.

This typical scenario poses a major difficulty—for purposes of security and protection of the individual inmate as well as of the prisoner population and staff as a whole, an initial classification interview should take place immediately after commitment and initial processing (if the inmate is committed on the late night shift, the interviewing can wait until the morning). The reason for this seemingly strict standard is that current experience in jails throughout the country is showing that more and more serious assaults and suicide attempts occur within the first day or two after commitment. To be effective, even the objective criteria used for the initial housing assignment by the jail's booking officer in lieu of a classification interview need to be examined and interpreted carefully.

For example, even though a new inmate may be 18 (an adult), male, awaiting trial on a rather serious charge, with a high bond, he may nonetheless also be a first-time offender, ignorant in the ways of the jailhouse, naive, and a soft, fuzzy-faced kid. In other words, if mistakenly housed in a unit with more sophisticated and experienced inmates, he may well be a mark for a homosexual attack. Similarly, New York City's jails have graphically learned that members of a certain ethnic group, if on drugs at the time of commitment, may be quiet, docile, and cooperative during the intake process but are also depressed and hyperanxious to a suicidal extreme. This fact may not be discerned until it is too late, unless a classification interview takes place shortly after reception into the institution. Once this initial interview has taken place, it is perfectly appropriate to wait until other pertinent information about an individual can be assembled before holding a more intensive classification session.

If the jail employs a part- or full-time classification officer, this person is usually considered to be part of the "treatment" or rehabilitation staff. If the size of the inmate traffic warrants, this individual would spend all of his or her time interviewing prisoners and obtaining, assembling, and analyzing whatever information is available on individual inmates. Where this is not a full-time activity, the same employee may also do some counseling or perform some other rehabilitation-related function.

In most small jails, however, there are neither classification personnel nor rehabilitation personnel due to budgetary and staffing limitations. Therefore, it is imperative that the booking officer, who would be the person making housing assignments in such jails, be given adequate training and guidelines with which to make appropriate initial classification decisions.

If the institution uses a committee system for classification purposes, the committee would normally meet once or twice a week. In the larger jails, this body would be chaired by a deputy warden; in other facilities, by the highest ranking officer on the guard force. One other member would normally be a member of the rehabilitation staff, with a third member coming from either the security or rehabilitation specialities. Committees of larger than three members in a jail have a tendency to become dysfunctional. There is also the possibility of "spending $50,000 on a $50 case."[8] In other words, an individual's needs, security status, etc. may be sufficiently obvious that there is no need to tie up considerable staff time on indepth analysis and profound deliberations. Each individual should be accorded the time and amount of consideration the facts of his or her situation indicate and warrant. In a number of jails, the findings of either the classification officer or a classification committee are merely recommendations and are forwarded to the institution's administrator for final approval and action.

As an offender's behavior and situation change, often a change in one or more aspects of his or her classification is appropriate. This *reclassification* function should also be performed by the classification officer or classification committee to ensure organizational continuity and effect a clearly recognizable locus within the jail for the making of such decisions. A well-organized jail will automatically make provisions for periodic review of the custody and program status of inmates who will be spending more than three or four months in confinement.

An additional duty given to the classification system by an increasing number of jail administrators is that of screening and recommending candidates for work, training, and educational release programs. This is a logical delegation, since presumably the classification process has developed a considerable amount of pertinent information about individual offenders and, through reclassification, has kept abreast of recent progress and developments on a case-by-case basis. However, it is important that clearly stated and defined criteria be provided the classification committee or officer as a guide by which to interpret the information available within the framework of the program's goals, objectives, and specific requirements.

In order for any system of classification to be effective, it is vital that the basic jail activities be organized in such a way as to allow for consistent implementation of classification recommendations. For instance, if the security designations "maximum," "medium," and "minimum" are to have any real meaning, separate housing units, different degrees of freedom of movement, variations in the types of work assignments to be given, etc. should be established. The more alternatives available for placement and programming of inmates within a jail, the more sophisticated and valuable the classification process can be. However, despite security designation, to assign someone, for example, to the first convenient and available bed, regardless of its location, defeats the entire purpose of classification. Likewise, if the jail has few or no programs, it is absurd to have a committee developing recommendations for programmatic involvement that can never be implemented. If sweeping the cellblock corridor is *the* program, there is no need to waste staff time to determine the obvious.

It is apparent, then, that to a large extent the effectiveness of classification is dependent on the overall resources available within and to the jail. An expansion of the number and types of programs available, for instance, increases the potential value of and need for an efficient classification process. Classification, therefore, must be integrated within the jail's organization and structure as an essential element of both the security and rehabilitation functions to achieve its maximal potential.

Operation of a Classification Program

The Dade County (Miami), Florida Jail has instituted a sensible and pragmatic approach to classification in a set of circumstances made complex by the large number of commitments to the facility. People booked into the jail in the evening and early morning hours are placed in temporary holding cells. If not taken to a magistrate's hearing the following morning, they are promptly interviewed by the jail's inmate assignment personnel. These interviews are conducted seven mornings per week.

In addition to obtaining the information necessary to make proper cell and work assignments, these initial interviews serve several other purposes.

The assignment (classification) officer uses this opportunity to give the inmate a brief orientation to the jail. This orientation includes the issuance and explanation of a pamphlet containing the facility's basic rules and regulations, as well as such important offender concerns as visiting hours and procedures. Information gathered through this interview is entered on an appropriate form and serves as a basis upon which to update and build a comprehensive store of information on the individual.[9]

During the interview, *special consideration is given to such matters as appearance, health, attitude and intelligence*. These items are vitally important in arriving at the proper classification and cell location. It is also during the interview that a determination is made to refer an inmate to the social workers for a family problem; to the labor officer as a trusty or day worker; to the medical office for medical problems; or to counselor for any other problem.[10]

The salient features of such a classification procedure are the timeliness, the various purposes achieved during the interview saving more staff time than if each task were performed on separate occasions; the obtaining and recording of data pertinent to making efficient classification decisions; and the identification of major inmate problems and the subsequent, immediate referral of the person to the appropriate rehabilitation staff member for assistance. Once these major problems have been resolved, there is time to deal with other treatment needs. But, for example, a newly committed inmate who is worried about how his family will eat while he is in jail will hardly concentrate on programmatic participation within the institution until his primary concern has been resolved. This is a problem-oriented approach to rehabilitation, which can be entirely appropriate, particularly in a short-term facility such as a jail.

Based on the information gained in the interview, the assignment officers at the Dade County Jail are able to make a prompt decision on custody status and housing assignment and have also identified and, through referral to proper inhouse resources, initiated resolution of significant program needs of the inmates. More extensive diagnosis and analysis can await the development of other pertinent information concerning the inmate, his or her background, and problems.

Tenets Underlying a Classification System

Having looked at the organizational and operational aspects of a classification program, it is appropriate to delineate the actual underlying system upon which such efforts should be based. Since the goal of classification is to separate offenders for both security and rehabilitation purposes, it is essential that some basic criteria be established to serve as guidelines for jail staff. As a basic rule of thumb, the following groups should be separated from the general inmate population. This "separation" does not imply any punitive measures; it merely signifies that the particular needs or characteristics of the group either call for some sort of special handling or pose a distinct or potentially serious problem for the jail.

Women

Women should obviously be housed in a separate area of the jail. This area should be supervised by female employees at all times. Every effort should be made to ensure that the women have the same programmatic, recreational, and visiting opportunities as the rest of the jail's population. To that end, a few institutions have made certain activities, such as academic classes, coeducational. The main objectives underlying the separation of women are to prevent wholescale sexual activity in the jail and to protect female inmates from sexual abuse.

Juveniles

Juveniles, if at all possible, should not even be in a jail. Detention centers that are designed, staffed, and programmed to meet the special needs of youths and a system of foster and group homes should be established to handle juveniles who require placement outside of their homes prior to adjudication by the juvenile court. If such facilities do not exist in a given community, thereby mandating jail commitment, under no circumstances should juveniles be intermingled with adult prisoners. The special nutritional needs of youngsters should be met and a full range of appropriate activities provided. To accomplish the latter, coordination with various youth service agencies is often very helpful. Perhaps the greatest service the jail can provide to a juvenile prisoner is to see to it that "every effort [is] made to expedite the disposition of the juvenile's case."[11]

Mentally Ill

Mentally ill people do not belong in jail, but rather in hospitals or other similar specialized facilities. Jails were never designed, equipped, or staffed to properly handle such individuals. But if mentally disturbed people are legally committed to the jail, the facility must nonetheless deal with them. They should be accorded extremely close supervision as a precautionary measure to prevent them from harming themselves or others. The jail should attempt to effect the transfer of such inmates to appropriate mental health facilities as expeditiously as possible. If this cannot be accomplished, however, the jail should make arrangements for such people to be seen by psychiatrists as soon as possible in order to obtain professional advice on the best methods of handling them. Such individuals should also be seen regularly by the jail physician. The primary objectives in this type of situation are to ensure the safety of these inmates and of those with whom they come into contact in the most humane manner possible. With the advent of various drugs, which should always and only be prescribed by a physician and administered in strict accordance with his or her instructions, physical restraints may not be necessary except in the most extreme cases. Within the boundaries of ensuring safety and common sense, the jail should in no way take any action that would at all aggravate the already strained mental condition.

Alcoholics

Ideally alcoholics should be taken to detoxification centers in the community and then afforded appropriate residential or outpatient treatment for their affliction. St. Louis, Missouri was an initiator of this type of alternative to dumping drunks in jail and overburdening the criminal justice system with them—a practice that accomplished nothing for the alcoholic. A number of other communities, either copying the St. Louis model or devising programs designed to meet unique local needs, have followed suit. In many areas, however, alcoholics are still incarcerated. In those instances, detoxification should be carried out under the supervision or general guidelines of the jail's physician. People experiencing delirium tremens should be transferred to a hospital immediately. Once detoxified, the alcoholic should be exposed to alcoholism education and counseling programs. Community groups, notably Alcoholics Anonymous, can be extremely helpful in the actual provision of services to inmates with acute alcoholism problems. Community mental health centers are another useful resource. In many areas there is substantial community concern about the alcoholism problem, which, with good public relations, can be tapped to obtain resources to establish or augment jail programs.

Narcotics Addicts

Narcotics addicts pose definite medical, programmatic, and security problems. The withdrawal process should be supervised by the jail's physician. Ideally, inmates should be transferred to a special ward at a local hospital during this period. However, few hospitals will, in fact, provide this service for the jail. During withdrawal, many addicts experience acute anxiety and/or depression, in addition to many physical maladies, and hence must be kept under close staff supervision. After withdrawal, addicts should be encouraged to participate in a narcotics treatment program, which would normally emphasize therapy or counseling. Various community narcotics treatment centers, agencies, and groups, such as Narcotics Anonymous, are helpful resources to call upon in designing and implementing programs. Because of the extreme nature of both the physical and psychological dependence that is an inherent part of the addiction, many incarcerated addicts will go to dire lengths to obtain narcotics. Particular attention must be given to properly securing all drugs in the jail's infirmary and to the prevention of drug smuggling via visiting or other contacts with the outside world.

Sex Offenders

Sex offenders should also be considered for separation from the general population. However, it should be noted that not all sex offenders pose a problem while incarcerated, e.g., voyeurs. Nonetheless, for the protection of the individual and of others in the jail, the nature of the sex offense and the offender's personality and background should be given serious consideration before a classification decision is made.

Escape Risks

Escape risks and other known security problem inmates should be identified and appropriate precautions taken. Normally, these people would be considered maximum custody and subject to closer supervision and more restricted movement within the jail than would be the general prisoner population. Their quarters and their persons would also be searched more frequently. They would be housed in the most secure area of the facility and, if given a job assignment, would work at a task that would not bring them into contact with actual or potential weapons. They should never be given access to an exit or outside area of the institution.

Special Medical Problems

Inmates with special medical problems in many instances should be housed separately, if not in the jail infirmary. Good jail management requires that newly committed inmates not be assigned to the general population until they have been medically cleared. If an inmate is found to have an infectious or contagious disease, such as syphillis or hepatitis, that person should obviously be kept in isolation until proper medical treatment has been effected. Handicapped inmates may need to be separated to protect them from being abused. Diabetics and epileptics will, of course, need special attention from the medical staff, although separate housing may not be required.

Separation of Sentenced and Unsentenced Prisoners

Unsentenced prisoners should be housed apart from sentenced inmates, although within the respective areas the same tenets of classification should apply. The fundamental reason underlying this separation is the difference in legal status between the two groups. Unsentenced prisoners have only been charged with a crime and, under the American system of justice, are thus considered to be innocent. Some will have the charges against them dismissed prior to trial, while others will probably secure their release on bond. Hence, there is a far greater flow of unsentenced as opposed to sentenced inmates in and out of the jail and consequently less stability in the unsentenced portion of the population.

In day-to-day terms, unsentenced prisoners for the most part must abide by the same rules and regulations as sentenced inmates. Unsentenced inmates, however, may not be compelled to work;[12] are not compelled to abide by strict haircut and grooming regulations, i.e., they may have long or unusual hair styles and/or beards as long as they maintain a suitable level of personal hygiene;[13] and, as part of their right to access to the courts and to assist in the preparation of their own defense, they must be allowed to make a reasonable number of phone calls.[14] Were the United Nations' standards ever to be fully implemented in the United States, there would be still other marked differences in the treatment of unsentenced prisoners.

Information Elements in Classification
Decisionmaking

To a considerable degree, classification decisionmaking can only be as good as the information upon which it is based. Hence, the more that is known about an individual offender, the more perceptive and accurate the classification actions concerning him or her can be. This presumes, of course, that the people doing the classifying are competent to analyze and diagnose this information. There are a number of elements common to most classification systems and several available sources external to the jail itself that can provide additional material concerning an individual offender and his or her background. The next several paragraphs indicate some of the major informational elements and sources that can be of substantial value to the classification officer or committee.

The *charge* obviously influences security considerations concerning an offender. First, the nature of the charge *may* indicate some aspect of the person's actual or potential behavior. Second, it is logical to assume that someone who is facing a serious charge with a possible lengthy sentence, if convicted, has more than the ordinary motivation to attempt to escape.

The charge per se, however, is not necessarily a firm guideline by which to classify. After all, the person may be wholly innocent of the charge, in which case it tells one absolutely nothing. Furthermore, with the exception of several sex offenses and escape and narcotics charges, the alleged crime for which the person is being detained is not a valid indicator of that individual's potential behavior while incarcerated. A person charged with petty larceny, for example, could possibly be extremely dangerous, if the opportunity and circumstances were presented for such behavior. Conversely, people serving life sentences in prisons for first degree murder, the most serious offense of all, generally pose fewer behavior problems than any offender group in the population.

Until adequate information is obtained about an offender, in order to exercise a proper degree of caution (even at the risk of being overly cautious), undue emphasis must be placed upon the charge in the initial classification process. Later on, the charge in combination with other information, such as an extensive prior record of violent crimes, may be significant in a particular classification decision.

In classifying sentenced prisoners for such community-oriented programs as work release, the charge does have definite significance, since it is incumbent upon jail officials to ensure public safety. A man who molests young girls, for example, may have a splendid behavioral record in an all male cellblock but, unless extensive diagnosis indicates to the contrary, may be a very poor risk in the community according to available research findings.

The amount of the *bond* in lieu of which the person is being detained is significant. If the bond is high, very few offenders will be able to secure release. A large bond is also usually indicative of the judge's assessment of the seriousness of the crime and the dangerousness of the offender. A high bond also provides a motivation to attempt escape. Similarly, a low bond signifies a relatively minor crime and a judicial view that the person being committed does not pose an especially serious threat to the community. It must be remembered that the jail staff is not present at the preliminary judicial proceedings at which bond is set nor is it privy to police reports of the crime. Initial classification, therefore, is somewhat a process of deductive reasoning based upon experience and the clues provided by such elements as charge and bond.

The *commitment paper*, which is the document given to the jail at the time of booking and serves as the legal authority to detain the person, in a few instances will contain special remarks by a judge or other court officer specifying certain conditions of confinement or conveying useful information. Such notations are extremely germane and helpful in the classification process but are relatively rare, especially in major cities, where a significant flow of people between the courts and the jail occurs. In one instance, a former inmate of a jail who had testified against other inmates in serious criminal proceedings was rearrested. The judge recognized the danger to the individual and intended but forgot to specify a condition of confinement to afford the person adequate protection. The day after commitment, the person was found murdered in his cell.[15]

If the offender had previously been committed to the jail, his or her *file pertaining to those prior commitments* should be retrieved immediately. The information in the file should have significant relevance for the instant classification process and save time and effort in developing anew the information already in the jail's possession. Records pertaining to prior adjustment and program participation in the jail are probably the most valid elements for classification purposes, especially when given whatever scant updating may be necessary, e.g., any education since release, most recent job held, etc.

The results of the *medical examination* or screening that should be given new commitments are certainly relevant to classification. In most instances, the examination will reveal nothing unusual; but in those cases in which a problem is indicated, the classification process should reflect this.

Prior criminal history should also be considered. When a person is booked into a jail, he or she is usually fingerprinted. The jail, in turn, should submit one copy of the prints to the FBI for its information and records purposes and request a copy of the person's FBI "rap sheet," i.e., record of prior arrests and dispositions. This information will give an indication of the person's criminal sophistication and may well provide clues as to potential behavioral patterns as well. Similar information may also be obtainable from local police or sheriff's departments.

Detainers (warrants from other jurisdictions indicating that they will assume custody of the person upon release from the jail) are also important for classification purposes. If an inmate is facing a serious charge somewhere else, even if he or she is only now being held on a minor offense, it may well provide motivation to escape.

The knowledge of the offender obtained from the *classification interview* should also be given serious weight.

If the person has ever served a sentence in an institution of the *correc-*

tions agency of the state in which the jail is located, any records, files, or similar material that may be obtained from that source would also be extremely helpful and serve to save staff time in redeveloping existing information. The availability of these records to jails is dependent upon the degree of cooperation between municipal, county, and state correctional officials.

A psychological inventory, such as the Minnesota Multi-Phasic Personality Inventory (MMPI), or similar psychological test should be administered to any person who will likely be at the jail for a month or more. The results of such psychological testing should be made available to the classification officer or committee.

Similary, an *educational achievement and nonverbal IQ tests* should be administered. The results would serve as a guide to the classification committee in determining the need and specific nature of any educational programming that may be appropriate for an individual.

A *vocational aptitude test* would also indicate prospective job assignments and training programming for the person while incarcerated.

Information obtained formally *from other agencies* can also be most relevant to the classification process. The local probation office, police department, welfare agency, school system, to name a few, may have had extensive prior contact with the inmate and developed a significant store of information about him or her. Tapping these resources, often by merely picking up the telephone, can save substantial staff time and result in the receipt of valuable knowledge that might not otherwise be obtained.

Other community sources, such as family members, minister, or employer, might also have useful contributions to make to the classification process. Some of them would obviously have a personal interest in cooperating with jail officials.

Staff observations are extremely significant inputs into any classification decision. The security staff sees the individual in a variety of roles and, in effect, lives with the inmate 24 hours per day. No other agency or part of the criminal justice system has this degree of extensive contact with the person. Similarly, observations of work supervisors, counselors, teachers, etc. are also important. The staff sees the inmate as he or she is, i.e., actual behavior, attitudes, and problems in both guarded, e.g., formal interviews with staff members, and unguarded moments. Hence, these observations given an experiential base to which other information elements may be applied and through which they may be interpreted. This total staff involvement in the classification process also serves to integrate it into the overall jail operation and helps to gain staff acceptance of and cooperation in implementing its decisions and recommendations. Such staff input and feedback are also valuable in evaluating the accuracy of classification decisions. In addition, such observations also provide an ongoing basis upon which to reconsider initial findings, if such action is indicated.

Classification Staffing Realities

Most jails do not have sufficiently adequate staffing to perform all the previously specified tasks involved in the classification process. While conducting an initial interview and making an assessment of such elements as charge, bond, and detainers pose few problems, testing and performing the follow-up required to obtain more detailed information about offenders may put a severe strain on the jail's limited personnel resources. In such instances, qualified volunteers and other community members can be recruited and trained to perform some of the testing and information-gathering functions. Ultimate interpretation of material and classification decision making should not and need not be delegated. In such a scenario, jail personnel still retain full authority, while the cooperating citizens make possible the acquisition of more complete information upon which to base decisions.

In supplementing existing staff, there is no reason, for example, why a volunteer educator from the community could not come into the jail once a week to test all newly committed inmates. Of course, if the jail has a full- or part-time teacher on the staff, such testing could be made a part of his or her duties. Similarly, if there is a university or community college in the area, an internship program could be developed that would provide the jail with additional help and simultaneously give students some practical vocational experience—all the while building a solid relationship with the school, thereby gaining a valuable ally in the community. There are a number of jails that use such approaches quite effectively and have consequently initiated sophisticated classification procedures and other programs that would never have been possible if the institution manager had relied solely on the personnel complement allotted via the appropriations process.

Conclusions

Classification is an essential part of the management and operation of a jail. A federal court recently recognized this fact by ordering the New York City Department of Corrections, which is responsible for the administration of all jails in the city, to institute a classification system[16]—one of several such decisions over the years. The adequacy of classification has substantial implications for the safety of inmates and staff, the security of the institution, and the efficacy of rehabilitation programs.

A basic, initial classification procedure should be commenced at the same time or as soon as possible thereafter as the commitment of the inmate to the jail. A more detailed diagnosis, analysis, and classification action can await the development of a more complete personal history of the offender, the results of testing, and the compilation of other relevant information. The knowledge garnered from such a process is a significant factor in the jail's handling of offenders and in ensuring that appropriate use is made of jail and community resources in addressing the needs and problems of inmates. In brief, it would be safe to assert that one of, if not *the,* key difference between a colonial-style human warehouse and a modern, well-managed jail is the existence of a thorough, ongoing classification system for all inmates.

5 How to Inaugurate Programs Now

We run a salvage business, not a junkyard.

Warden John D. Case

Why Try to Rehabilitate?

As contrasted with those numerous, anonymous perpetrators of crime in the streets, sentenced offenders in jails and prisons constitute a known body of criminals. If for whatever reason they have found it either desirable or mistakenly necessary to commit crime while free in the community, it is only reasonable to assume that if no steps are taken between the time of sentence and eventual release to affect a positive change in attitude and behavior, these same people will again revert to crime when back among us. From the perspective of resource management in a field with so many imponderables and unknowns, mere common sense mandates that major efforts be undertaken to achieve appropriate individual change in a serious attempt to reduce the proliferation of crime. While vast sums of money are expended on searching out and combatting criminals who remain either unidentifiable to the authorities or unconvicted by the criminal justice system, known contributors to the crime problem languish in neglectful isolation in jail and no attempts are made to deal with this past and potential threat to public safety. Apparently the public psyche is mollified by a court conviction and the adoption of the subsequent "out of sight, out of mind" attitude, which would be almost sensible were it not for the fact that these offenders will soon be out on the streets again. A perfect opportunity for effective prevention of future crime is thereby missed.

Within this framework, most jails function as human warehouses, merely satisfied to achieve containment of committed offenders. Beyond confinement, the major preoccupation of jailers is to provide the minimum essentials for maintaining human life. Even a cursory examination of the files of seasoned, career criminals in long-term state and federal prisons will reveal that a substantial majority of these individuals started out as petty criminals confined in local jails. This fact in combination with the few existing jail recidivism studies and the empirical experience of criminal justice officials serves as striking evidence of the abject failure of jails to change or even deter their prisoners from a life of crime.

Advocates of jail reform are frequently labeled "do-gooders," fuzzy-headed thinkers, or "soft" on criminals at the expense of the victims. While reform efforts, to be sure, may be partially motivated by humane considerations, they are essentially based on a recognition that traditional methods of dealing with convicted offenders have failed miserably to accomplish any constructive purpose other than the perpetuation of some very expensive warehouses with steel bars. The call for initiation or expansion of rehabilitation programs focuses, naturally, on the offender, but the ultimate concern is for the next potential victim. The jail administrator can do little to ease the harm done to past victims but is in a position to prevent future crimes and a continuation and growth of offender criminality. If the prevailing approaches to jail administration were at all effective in achieving this goal, then attempts to improve jails would be misguided, for there are a number of other serious social problems that also cry out for immediate attention and action. But current jail administration is not effective, and therein lies the essential tragedy of "business as usual" in the local jail.

Philosophical Base

In an attempt to realign the basic operations of a jail so as to address the rehabilitation objective as well as that of confinement, one paramount consideration must be recognized. The essence of successful rehabilitation of the offender resides in the ability to inculcate in the individual a functioning attitude of positive self-responsibility. Cutting through the morass of theories of criminal causation, one fact remains abundantly clear—with the exception of the de facto rare individual who commits a crime of conscience—a person who is convicted of a criminal offense has evidenced a lack of proper self-responsibility. People are in jail because they could not responsibly exercise normal freedoms in a socially acceptable manner. The "why" behind the action indicates what necessary steps must be taken to achieve the rehabilitation objective.

This fundamental consideration applies not just to rehabilitation but to jail administration as well. Frequently, improvements in a jail are staunchly criticized as creating a "country club" behind bars. Seemingly, regardless of inmate behavior, some institutions are perceived as providing "goodie" after "goodie" and privilege after privilege in the name of rehabilitation. In most cases, the "goodies" are merely bringing the jail up to the basic contemporary standards of human habitation. But it is true that some administrators will try to "buy" peace and order by constant accession to inmate demands and pressures. This is not a rehabilitation-oriented institution, but rather a "sweet jail." Just as in any community there is an equal and corresponding responsibility for every right or privilege, the same is also true in a well-managed jail. If abuse of opportunities and privileges occurs and is permitted to continue unabated, the goal of rehabilitation is frustrated and there will be eventual chaos in the facility.

Self-responsibility is often equated with or considered a function of emotional maturity. Regardless of chronological age, on a scale of emotional maturity most jail inmates would be functioning on the level of 12- to 14-year-olds. This statement is not intended to be derogatory, but rather to indicate the extent to which fundamental human needs, those which are essential for positive personality growth and development, have not been met for whatever reasons. Therefore, rehabilitation programs that are conducted within an environment that is essentially punitive and/or anonymously authoritative are doomed to failure. For such a milieu, by its very nature and intent, stunts personal growth and inhibits even a small degree of exercise of self-responsibility. If such authority is not carried out in too oppressive a fashion, it can be an effective means of control. However, it basically treats inmates as children, without providing any opportunity for positive human development.

In response to simplistically perceived offender needs, progressive administrators and reformers will often institute a variety of "programs." These programs may well address themselves to educational deficiencies, medical and religious needs, and other similar legitimate problems that inhibit the chances for ex-offender success in a complex society. However, learning a trade in great demand will not benefit an ex-offender in the long run, if he or she is continually late to work or punches the boss if the latter should attempt to correct a mistake. Obviously, social skills must also be imparted.

A climate must be created in which programs can be meaningful. This, in and of itself, makes a significant contribution to rehabilitation. Such a climate requires a high degree of human interaction between staff and inmates that is predicated upon fundamental concepts of respect and human dignity. Staff interest, as manifested by recognition of offenders as individuals and a genuine willingness to engage in informal problem-solving and guidance, is the essential human element that makes a jail an agent of rehabilitation. Within such an atmosphere, growth is supported and encouraged and actual programs reinforced. This approach does not mean that guards must become buddies with the inmates or compromise their authority and the jail's security. In essence, the establishment and maintenance of such an environment requires staff to merely recognize that prisoners are also human beings and to treat them as such, using the common sense and good judgment appropriate to the jail function. Such staff/inmate relationships can often provide a motivation for individuals to change.

No program can change anyone unless the individual recognizes a need to alter behavioral patterns and desires to do so. Once an inmate has the motivation, then programs can be of significant benefit in completing and enhancing the fundamental change process. Far too often, governmental programs of every type give the impression of processing numbers through the service delivery line in total neglect of the initial support, encouragement, and motivational needs of the participants. Given the former and a little constructive advice, the individual would probably be able to discover and obtain the needed services on his or her own. An atmosphere in which a respect for other people is informally conveyed, particularly by example, is a major stimulus to the development and growth of an offender's personality, which is at the heart of any successful effort to achieve a positive alteration of attitudes and behavior.

Calling attention to the importance of creating an environment that is conducive to growth and change in no way diminishes the value of formalized, structured programs, for relevant programs can impart "tools" that are pragmatically vital for successful living in the community. A mature, self-responsible person can only properly utilize skills and talents if he or she possesses them. A certain minimal level of educational attainment, a vocational skill, knowledge of ways to properly utilize leisure time, and so on are all essential elements of successfully coping in society, and can be learned while in jail. The range of program needs in a jail is extensive.

One must remember that most inmates are "losers"—they have failed at virtually everything they have ever tried. They have dropped out of school, have had severe marital problems, have been repeatedly fired from jobs (if they could find employment to begin with), etc. They have even failed at crime, otherwise they would not be in jail. When one reflects that recent studies have shown, for example, that "an adult burglar has only one chance in 412 of going to jail for any single job,"[1] and that many inmates are in jail as a result of their first or second attempt at crime, the inevitable conclusion is that somewhere there are a goodly number of successful criminals for whom crime does pay. Successful criminals do not wind up in jail—they frequently do not get caught. If they do get caught, they are financially able to hire sufficiently talented attorneys to win acquittal. In general, however, they suffer a fate other than confinement. These are the individuals who pose a real threat to society, far more so than the vast majority of the people in jails and prisons. Institutions only get the ones who fail.

Introduction to "Programs"

In reality, then, one of the functions of jails is to turn "losers" into "winners," and in the fulfillment of this task programs have a major role to perform. The remainder of this chapter contains a "how to" guide to jail programming.[a] The major programs found in well-managed jails are discussed, their potential benefits assessed, and suggestions relative to inaugurating these programs are described. Special emphasis is placed upon resources, available in most communities, that may be of substantial assistance in program design and operation. This material reflects progressive practices that have been successfully tried in jails and is not mere theoretical abstraction. The actual implementation of these programs would represent a significant improvement in the vast majority of American jails and, drawing as they do on existing community resources, are economically feasible for even the most underfunded facility.

Social Services

Any social service unit in a jail must be carefully planned to ensure that its objectives and activities coordinate well with programs such as pretrial release, probation, legal services, and others. There almost inevitably will be some overlap, but it should be minimized.

Help in a Crisis

Perhaps the most crucial service to render in a jail is crisis intervention. Much of this effort will be directed to newly admitted prisoners. It may include contacts with families, relatives, and other interested people, such as former employers. In general, the focus is upon minimizing the disruption that occurs as a result of arrest and confinement—disruption that affects not only the inmate but family, friends, and employer.

An important byproduct of the crisis intervention function is the positive response it evokes from prisoners, their families, and friends. For most of them, arrest and confinement is a crisis, and assistance from a trained staff member or volunteer is a welcome experience. It has a very positive impact on inmate morale by reducing the frustration and feeling of helplessness that, when it becomes widespread among inmates, can turn minor irritations into critical problems and increase the likelihood of fights, clashes with staff, and other disturbances.

[a]The following material on jail programming (Visiting and Suicide Prevention excepted) has been adapted and, in several sections, reprinted from "A Handbook on Jail Programs" (Washington, D.C.: National Sheriffs' Association, 1974), pp. 13-21, 25-27, with the kind permission of the National Sheriffs' Association, which was responsible for its preparation under the auspices of the United States Department of Justice, Law Enforcement Assistance Administration, Grant Award No. 73-ED-99-0002. The "Handbook" was cowritten by myself, E. Eugene Miller, and James E. Murphy under contract to the Association. It appears here as a gracious courtesy of the Association and in no way implies Association or LEAA endorsement of any of the views or opinions stated elsewhere in this chapter or book.

Crisis intervention may consist, for example, of calling a friend of the prisoner to arrange for his automobile to be taken home, a paycheck to be picked up, arrangements for child care to be made. Beyond that, the social service staff serves as liaison between the prisoner and the community. The staff can serve a very useful function as a referral source for the prisoner's family. For families at all economic levels, arrest of the breadwinner is traumatic, creating a social crisis and often an immediate financial one. Many do not know where to turn for public assistance and go from one agency to another in search of help. The staff of the jail social service unit can be of significant benefit by referring such families to appropriate sources of aid.

Other Functions

Beyond crisis intervention, the social service unit should provide basic counseling services to confined people. Often, what would appear to be relatively simple problems, easily resolved, are manifest contributors to individual criminality. If staffing and budget permit, group counseling is also a desirable service for this unit. Since there are usually few activities in most jails at night and on weekends, the unit can accomplish much during these times. When faced with the realities of a stark cellblock, an individual often desires someone in whom to confide and is more receptive at these times to counseling efforts than when he or she is distracted by involvement in various activities. By rotating off-hour coverage among the unit's staff, the desired programmatic effect is obtained without being considered an opprobrious assignment.

Few, if any, jails have the budgetary resources to hire full-time psychiatrists. This situation is only slightly improved as it pertains to psychologists. Ideally, a jail should have both of these disciplines represented on the staff. Pragmatically, the best hope of obtaining such services resides in the jail administrator's ability to "borrow" from other community agencies, such as a mental health clinic, or secure funds for this purpose from foundations and/or federal grants. With the addition of such personnel to the staff, other types of treatment, including individual and group psychotherapy, are possible. This capability can also be used to bolster diagnostic and classification functions, which would ensure proper programmatic prescription and assignment. In view of current trends in the mental health field, a substantial amount of a staff psychiatrist's time should be spent as a resource person to other staff, providing advice on difficult cases and training all personnel in order to upgrade basic counseling and human relations skills.

Whatever the organization and funding base of the unit, it is important that the jail, as part of the criminal justice system, have available the information gathered by agencies, usually the police, who had contact with the prisoner prior to his arrival at the jail and pass that information along to others (e.g., pretrial diversion program staff, probation officers, etc.) as well as the pertinent data and information recorded at the jail. This will help the entire local criminal justice system avoid the problem that probably is the second most costly to the system today—the enormous duplication of effort expended by several agencies in the system that repeatedly gather the same information about the same people. (The most costly problem is the unnecessary institutionalization of people who present no threat to the community or to themselves.)

Assistance from Other Agencies

At this point, there is no standard organizational arrangement for a jail social service unit except that it should have a single administrative head who reports to the jail administrator. The social service staff may be funded by and be part of the local community mental health center or clinic, welfare office, vocational rehabilitation department, mental health service, or Model Cities project. Possibly it can be funded through the state law enforcement planning agency (SPA) with LEAA funds. The disadvantage of grant funding is that it is usually short term (up to three years) and subject to the availability of funds.

Regardless of the organizational arrangement, basic services may be greatly benefited if augmented by one or more full- or part-time staff from one of the above agencies. Such staff can either be available on a scheduled or referral basis, responding when the jail social service unit identifies a potential candidate for the services they offer.

Private funds have been utilized in some jurisdictions to fully or partially finance the social service unit. The private sources for funds are usually the United Fund or Community Chest. Among sources of service are family service agencies, church-based agencies such as Lutheran, Catholic, or Jewish social service agencies, and private mental health groups.

Specialized services are also available in many jurisdictions from local agencies concerned with drug and alcohol abuse and with the care, treatment, and training of the mentally retarded. Help may also come from organizations that deal with special populations, such as people with birth defects, hearing or sight problems, and those with specific illnesses or disabilities such as multiple sclerosis or muscular dystrophy, even though the need for these latter services is ordinarily quite rare.

Another important service available in most communities is employment counseling. Several states have set up a section of the employment service specifically for offenders—Comprehensive Offender Manpower Services (COMPS). COMPS has access to all specialized services provided or funded by the employment service, including vocational testing and evaluation, job bank, and employment counseling, as well as monetary benefits for those who are eligible.

In making referrals to other agencies, common faults are (1) not providing adequate descriptions of the problem that is the basis for the referral; (2) lack of follow-up while the defendant is receiving assistance from the accepting agency; and (3) lack of follow-up after completion of the service. Resolution of the second and third faults is essential in refining criteria for future referrals. In some instances, it is also helpful if the jail staff continues contact with the individual referred on a supportive basis. This, however, should be worked out with the agency from which the individual is receiving service, since continued contact by jail staff might be perceived as interference by the other agency.

Special Offenders

The term *special offenders* generally refers to those individuals who by nature of their comparatively small numbers or the uniqueness of their problems are of special concern to jailers. Depending on individual points of view, the list of special offenders could be lengthy indeed. For our purposes, only the major categories of special offenders found in many jails will be discussed. These are juveniles, the mentally ill, alcoholics, and drug addicts.

The Juvenile Prisoner

Only under highly unusual circumstances should juveniles be confined in a jail. Modern practice dictates that juveniles in need of detention prior to juvenile court proceedings be held in a separate detention facility designed, programmed, and staffed to meet their specific needs. Unfortunately, this is not the situation in some places, and thus the jail must deal with this type of offender.

In dealing with juveniles an inviolable rule is that under no circumstances should juveniles be housed or mingled with adult prisoners. The possible negative influence and other dangers to the well-being of such juveniles are obvious. Potential abuse has prompted a number of states to pass laws that forbid mixing juveniles and adults in confinement.

Like an adult, a juvenile may be in need of a wide range of services, such as medical care, social services, recreation and leisure time activities, religion, or education. Because of the rapid growth and abundant energy that characterize teenagers, the actual "mix" of activities may be somewhat varied.

One of the sometimes disastrous side-effects of detention for a juvenile is that he or she is suddenly taken out of school and, even if released within a few weeks, falls behind the rest of the class and is thus in danger of being left back or receiving a "gentleman's promotion." Coordination should be established with the local school system to ensure that the appropriate books, materials, and assignments are provided to enable the jailed youngster to keep up. Teachers are made available to detained youngsters by many schools.

Similar links should also be established with other appropriate community agencies, since frequently one of the major factors contributing to the individual's delinquency is the home situation. These agencies should help both the youngster in dealing with that environment and the family in making whatever adjustments may be necessary.

Shattering as the first clang of the steel grill may be for an adult, it is even more traumatic for a teenager. Thus she or he presents a pressing need for crisis intervention on the part of the jail's social service program.

The Mentally Ill Prisoner

People who are seriously mentally ill or retarded should quite obviously be in a mental health facility and not a jail. Unfortunately, reality often dictates that these people, at least temporarily, wind up on the jailer's doorstep instead of in the hospital. Mentally ill people should not be housed with the general jail population, and steps should be taken to ensure that they do not cause serious harm to themselves or others. The jail physician should be consulted as soon as possible and his professional advice sought on the best methods of treating and managing the individual until other arrangements can be made. For the individual who is violent or shows tendencies toward violence, there are tranquilizing drugs which, of course, should be prescribed by a physician and administered scrupulously under his direction and instructions. There is no excuse today for shackling, manacling, and similar practices used in years past. Extreme isolation can often serve to heighten the existing mental problems, and therefore the social services staff should be active in assisting the individual.

The Suicidal Prisoner

Suicides have become an increasing problem in jails. The prime rule of thumb is that any person who is a suicide threat should be immediately transferred to an appropriate hospital facility. Regrettably, through no fault of the jail's, this is very often not possible without considerable delays; and therefore, the jail staff must deal with the problem. There is no infallible guideline for determining in advance who may attempt suicide. Common sense, however, would indicate that people with a known pattern of suicide attempts while incarcerated, those who seriously start verbalizing a desire to end their own lives, and normally active and alert individuals who suddenly enter into a highly depressed, almost catatonic state warrant close observation.

Every jail should have a "suicide watch" procedure, consisting of several elements. The inmate should be immediately interviewed and evaluated by a competent mental health professional; if prompt transfer to a hospital is impossible, the individual should be separated from the general population. *All staff* should be alerted to the situation. This alert should include the recommendations and advice of the mental health worker. Counseling and medical staff should frequently talk with the inmate both to provide whatever services may help alleviate the problem and to further gauge the potential for inflicting self-harm. The person's access to implements that might be used in a suicide attempt should be stringently limited and closely supervised. Many jails have now instituted a procedure whereby an officer must check on the inmate at least every 15 minutes or half-hour, which, in a particularly overcrowded and understaffed facility, may be the most frequent guaranteed observation possible. However, in those jails with a close-circuit television capability, a small, portable camera mounted on a tripod outside the cell or room permits the central control officer continual monitoring of the situation. While this may seem to be a rank invasion of privacy, it alleviates the need for the continual administration of comatose-type drugs, which is not always possible or advisable anyway, and inhumane physical restraints. These steps should substantially reduce the opportunities for suicide attempts until such time as the individual can be transferred to the appropriate facility.

The Alcoholic Prisoner

Alcoholics also pose a special problem. Many alcoholics have extreme physical problems caused by the neglect of health, nutrition, and hygiene that often accompanies alcoholism. A "drying out" process may be necessary. If it is apparent that an onslaught of the DT's is imminent, the individual should be transferred to a hospital.

Special programs for the alcoholic can be provided in the jail. For example, Alcoholics Anonymous is most cooperative in holding meetings at jails and providing numerous services to alcoholics in jail populations. In several jurisdictions, state and/or local agencies charged with treating alcoholics have either staffed or funded alcoholism projects in jails.

Coordination and cooperation with community mental health centers may also provide a source of tangible programmatic assistance for alcoholic offenders. Alcoholism is a problem to which many people in the community are sympathetic; and consequently, more people are inclined to help offenders afflicted with serious drinking problems. In one county, a wealthy industrialist paid the salary of a psychologist to work with alcoholics in jail. In another, a local citizens group paid for the services of a full-time psychiatrist for such clients.

The Drug Addicted Prisoner

Drug addicts (as opposed to drug users) also present special problems. Ideally, addicts in withdrawal should be transferred to local hospitals, since very few jails are properly staffed to deal with this medical problem. Again, reality mandates that frequently withdrawal must be accomplished at the jail. During this period, addicts should be separated from the general population and placed in the infirmary area. To the extent possible, this process should be medically supervised and directed. The withdrawal process can either cause or aggravate medical problems and just letting the person go "cold turkey" without being under a physician's care can be a dangerous practice.

As with alcoholics, special programs can be brought into the jail for the benefit of addicts. When New York City instituted a methadone detoxification service in its massive detention institutions in 1971, it was a pleasant surprise to the correctional officers as well as the medical staff to find that the program had a dramatic effect in reducing the tensions in the jails, especially those between staff and prisoners. Narcotics Anonymous and similar organizations can be quite helpful in providing a wide range of services for addicts. Community mental health centers and various state and local programs for addicts can be tapped as program resources as well.

Conclusion

In the ideal world, several of the foregoing offender categories would be diverted prior to reaching the jail. But, as is only too well known to the officer on the midnight shift, the jail must deal with—and probably will for some time to come—the perennial problem of "Whadya do with the drunken sailor?" and others who need care that the jail is not really equipped to furnish. Proper procedures need to be established with professional guidance and assistance, and the progressive jail will establish specialized treatment programs drawing heavily on existing community resources.

Education

Education programs in jails are, by the very nature of the potential student's short-term stay as a detentioner or sentenced misdemeanant, different in focus and emphasis than they would be in virtually any other type of institution. Nonetheless, the need is just as great. Numerous studies have shown that jail inmates function at slightly below the sixth grade level. Given the demands of today's world, this means that they are practically illiterate. At the same time, they have the same average IQ as the population in the free world.

The benefits and importance of education in any rehabilitation program are obvious. An increase in educational levels may well help an individual get and keep a job, increase his or her ability to function in an increasingly complex world, and lead to an increase in self-esteem, among other advantages.

Few inmates, if any, will be in the jail long enough to benefit from a traditional method of education, with an emphasis on fixed curriculum and terms. The college programs for long-term prisoners are not possible in jails. Hence, education in the jail becomes a distinct challenge to the administrator's creativity.

Resources for the Jail Program

Several good resources are available to help a jail start and maintain an education program. Sometimes the local school district will provide teachers, books, and supplies directly, in the belief that it is obligated to provide for the educational needs of the jail population. If nothing else, the local school system will almost always supply texts and materials for an education program. Volunteer teachers may be available from a variety of sources—local public and private school faculties, faculties of community and 4-year colleges and universities, and the community as a whole. These people may be recruited, screened, and oriented as one would with any volunteer. Of course, if the jail has the budget and positions for a regular school program, then the need to beat the bushes in the community for teachers is for the most part eliminated.

Content of the Educational Program

Design of courses and curriculum calls for considerable creativity and flexibility. For those inmates who have had a fair amount of formal schooling, arrangements can be made for a "cram" course of tutoring by volunteers to help them qualify for a GED (high school equivalency diploma). Usually, arrangements can easily be made with the state board of education to administer and grade the tests and award the diplomas.

For the others, primary emphasis should be placed on classes that will immediately help them function more adequately in the community. Consequently, the three R's should receive a good deal of attention. This is not to say that a wide variety of classes in many different subjects cannot be offered, depending on the interests of the inmates and the availability of teachers and space. A main responsibility and goal of any educational effort in jails should be to concentrate on those individuals who have difficulty functioning because of a lack of even the most rudimentary skills of formal education, such as making change and reading street signs and bus schedules.

Prior to placement in an educational program, each inmate/student should be tested to determine the level at which she or he is actually functioning. Many times an inmate has told an interviewer that he or she "went to the eleventh grade", when in reality he or she is reading on a third or fourth grade level. This information is necessary for the teacher to be able to plan classes and a level of instruction to meet the needs of the students. If the material presented is over their heads, they will soon become frustrated and feel inadequate. Individualized instruction buttressed with programmed instruction and materials has proved to be very successful. The traditional classroom approach has quite often failed in this kind of situation because the "students" are of such differing ages, levels of achievement, and interests. Furthermore, most have dropped out of school or been expelled or otherwise failed in the classroom. Being placed back in the same situation most frequently leads to repeated failure. Equally, however, if the material is below the level of the class, the "students" will become bored and lose interest.

Several other factors should be remembered when designing and running an educational program in a jail. Given the amount of idleness in most jails, once students are properly motivated, they will frequently outperform their free world counterparts. With few distractions and a need to keep occupied, students will spend far more time on assignments and in related work than will a typical high school teenager with a wide variety of other interests and diversions. Because of the high turnover in jail populations and, consequently, in classes at the jail, each lesson should be so designed that if a person went to just one class, he would carry some useful knowledge away with him. Each lesson thus becomes an entity in itself. To further this concept, a one-room schoolhouse approach can often be most helpful. The teacher can work with one inmate, explain a point, give an exercise in it, then move on to the next student. This approach enables the teacher to work with a number of students of different educational levels at the same time.

Texts and books pose a unique problem. One cannot realistically expect a grown man to return to his cell with a "Run, Dick, Run" book in his hands. Magazines, however, can be quite helpful. A careful search of newsstands reveals magazines on sports and similar subjects that are interesting to inmates and are using the most elementary to relatively advanced vocabularies.

Programmed learning (self-teaching) texts are also helpful. These allow students to progress at their own speeds and give immediate feedback on progress. One series of texts goes a long way because the inmates are working at different academic levels. Therefore, several inmates are working with the same set of books simultaneously. Other materials used in classes should be of a practical nature. For example, job application forms obtained from a local company or employment agency can be used in practicing reading or writing. Thus, if a person only learns how to read 50 words, that knowledge might be sufficient to get a job. In math, an income tax form or a newspaper ad about buying a car on time not only offers practical examples to illustrate points but also provides useful information on situations with which the inmate will come into contact upon release. In other words, it is necessary to make the effort to keep the students' interest and to provide them with usable skills, particularly when one realizes that, for whatever reason, these people did not make it in the traditional school system.

Space for classes can pose a real problem in those jails which were designed without programs in mind. Here, too, imagination and ingenuity are often necessary. In many jails, an office, dining room, or library can become a learning center and classroom at night. Better-planned space would, of course, be ideal, but real education is more the function of a skilled teacher and "turned on" students than of elaborate or expensive surroundings.

When an inmate/student approaches the day of release, some effort should be made to tell him where in the community he may continue his education. Perhaps, periodically, a representative of the local adult education program of the school system can come to the jail and either discuss this point with people nearing release or actually enroll them in programs. Hopefully, a good education program in a jail will be a start, not an end, to the learning process.

Health Services

Health services in jails constitute one of the most sensitive program areas. There is little public resistance to the provision of such services, but they present many problems. Poor medical and dental services usually are at or near the top of grievance lists of inmates involved in jail disturbances.

This is also the area about which the courts have recently been most firm in requiring adequate services, although until recently it was considered part of the inner workings of the jail and therefore subject to the "hands off" doctrine. One of the most far-reaching decisions on this issue handed down by a federal court held that the lack of adequate medical treatment and care afforded to prisoners in a particular institution violated their constitutional right to be free of cruel and unusual punishment. In summary, the court ordered that jail hospital services be improved to conform with standards and regulations required of community hospitals; that each jail hospital have written sanitation procedures approved by the medical director; that medical equipment be updated; that a minimum staffing proposal be filed; that officials ensure that every inmate in need of medical attention be seen by a qualified medical attendant and by a physician when necessary; and that a complete medical record for each prisoner be maintained. This decision marks the latest step of the courts in requiring that prisoners be afforded a level of medical care comparable to that provided in the community. Unfortunately, relatively few jails can now meet that standard.

The problem is complicated by the fact that many of those who are committed to jail are poor and have not usually had adequate health care prior to admission. Therefore, they have more health deficiencies and defects than the general population. It is not unusual to encounter jail inmates who have never visited a doctor or dentist.

Basic Health Services Required

Realistically, the jail cannot assume responsibility for all the health needs and deficiencies of all people committed to custody. There is, however, a minimum level of services that is generally agreed upon.

Every new prisoner should be examined to see if there are any open wounds or sores that require treatment or evidence of recent disease or body vermin. These and other symptoms, such as difficulty in breathing, swallowing, or other normal body functions, may be cause for immediate evaluation by a physician. Preferably, the arresting officer(s) will have performed this function. By short questions and answers, an attempt should be made to determine whether or not the prisoner is a drug addict or alcoholic who may soon start going through withdrawal or DT's. Care must obviously be taken to properly isolate and treat those people with such health problems as venereal diseases and hepatitis (which many addicts have without realizing it) in order to prevent the carriers from infecting others. The classification committee should know of any serious health problems so that no such mistake as assigning an active hepatitis carrier to kitchen duty will be made.

Staffing for Health Services

Ideally, a full-time physician and part-time dentist should be available, but this objective is unrealistic except for larger institutions. In addition to being available for emergencies, the physician should visit the jail regularly to examine newly admitted individuals, respond to prisoners' requests, make referrals, and provide follow-up treatment. Therefore, it is necessary for most jails to rely upon the local health officer or a contractual arrangement with a local physician.

Another alternative for securing a high level of medical care, especially in major metropolitan areas, is to make arrangements with a local university medical school to provide residents and interns under the close supervision of a physician/faculty member. Such agreements result in more medical personnel, the possibility of around-the-clock medical presence or, at the least, greater coverage, ensure the backup of the full resources of the medical school, and all at a significantly reduced cost to the jail. This approach, when used in combination with a regular, full-time jail physician and nurse(s), will enable the institution to fully meet its responsibility in providing for inmates' medical needs.

As in other areas, the health service program should be coordinated with, and utilize, other resources in the community, such as the local and state health departments, hospitals, clinics, medical, dental, and paramedical organizations. To the extent possible, the health program should have a very close relationship with, if not actually be a part of, the local public health program. If nothing else, local medical societies should be able to conduct surveys of existing medical programs at jails and suggest ways of improving them. Perhaps these same groups can suggest means of securing additional professional coverage. Recommendations coming from such influential professional organizations can lend added weight to any requests for increased funding for health services at jails.

Although not a substitute for physician services, adequate paramedical staff, such as nurses and medical technicians, should be employed to administer medical screening and rudimentary health services. They will be able to recognize symptoms of serious illnesses, distinguish between intoxication and other illnesses and injuries that result in similar symptoms (e.g., diabetic coma), and render first aid. It should be emphasized, however, that paramedical personnel must have a physician available to them for emergencies and that their screening is not a substitute for examination by a physician.

It is also important to have as many of the staff as possible take an approved first aid course, perhaps as part of their initial training. This type of training is invaluable in emergencies and has saved many lives.

Dental care should be made available to every inmate. Most jails follow the rule that detentioners qualify only for emergency dental work, while sentenced misdemeanants who will be in the jail for a while may get normal dental service. This rule is necessitated by the medical and dental budget of the jail, which is almost always too small.

Sick Call and Treatment

It is customary in many jails to have a specific "sick call" time. In others, this is not the case. In still others, there is more than one time during the day when inmates may be seen by the medical staff. The size and complexity of the jail operation, the staffing pattern, and the physical plant will influence selection of the arrangement that results in the best plan for delivery of health services in any particular jail.

There should be provision for isolation of prisoners suffering from contagious diseases. This can be accomplished in jail infirmaries. Those jails which have no adequately equipped infirmary usually have a standing arrangement with a local hospital. The advantages and disadvantages of each arrangement must be worked out on an individual basis in terms of costs, distance, and availability of custodial supervision. There will be situations in which hospitalization must be arranged for serious emergencies that are beyond the capability of the jail, and provision must be made for emergency ambulance services and hospitalization. In some jurisdictions, hospitals have set up "locked wards" that incorporate the necessary physical security for handling prisoners.

Records and Supplies

Medical records, another essential component of the program, should be maintained in accord with established professional standards. Of particular importance is a record of the inmate's condition at admission (including cuts, bruises, or other evidence of illness or injury), reasonable prior medical history, any illness or injury during confinement and treatment thereof, and condition at the time of release. Inmates should not maintain or have access to medical records because of the nature of the information contained in them and the opportunity to alter their own or other inmates' records.

Medical supplies should be kept securely locked and be inventoried regularly. They should be dispensed only by the physician or, upon his orders, by adequately trained staff. Inmates should be given medication one dose at a time and be required to take it in the presence of a staff member.

One of the most difficult decisions for a jailer to make is what to do with the inmate who becomes ill at 3 a.m. when no medical staff is on duty. This is probably the most unfair demand placed on the jailer since by everyone's admission he is not trained to perform this function. Common sense should prevail. If the jailer has any doubts about the seriousness of the inmate's condition, he should immediately contact the jail physician or arrange for transport to the emergency room of a hospital. Many inmates have died because of a well-meaning "I'll make sure you see the doctor in the morning." When dealing with such a serious and complex area as health services, "play it safe" is a sound rule of thumb.

6

Other Worthwhile Program Services and Volunteers

How you gonna rehabilitate me, Warden, when I ain't been habilitated yet?
An Anonymous Inmate

Recreation and Leisure Services

One of the major architectural failings of most jails today is that they have inadequate space—or none at all—for recreation and leisure services. Yet jail administrators are considered to be both morally and legally responsible for the physical and mental health of inmates. Certainly, recreation is an essential element in meeting this responsibility. In many instances, however, because of lack of space, equipment, and improper jail design, provision for adequate recreation takes considerable creativity and ingenuity on the part of the jail staff.

Ideally, a jail would have a sufficient budget to permit full- or part-time personnel to organize and supervise a regular program of recreation and other leisure activities. In the overwhelming majority of jails, however, this is not the case. Frequently a staff member is assigned this task as an additional duty and is given a very restricted budget with which to purchase necessary supplies.

Leisure services can be an important support to effective custody, as well as to the rehabilitation effort. Frequently, lack of proper use of leisure time helps get a person into trouble while in jail. Subsequent to release, this problem will increase. If an inmate can be exposed to or taught an enjoyable, constructive way to use leisure, it can be of considerable benefit in helping him or her make a successful adjustment in the community.

Television and Radio

Television has today become a staple element in any institutional recreation program. The sets should be placed in areas to which the inmate population has ready access and should be enclosed to prevent tampering or instant repairs by the resident "expert" in the population. Hours during which

Some of the material in this chapter is also reprinted from and, in several instances, adapted from the National Sheriffs' Association's "Handbook on Jail Programs," (pp. 22-24, 28-32, 39, 40, 43-46) with permission.

81

television may be watched should be clearly posted, with occasional exceptions made for special events. It is interesting to note that when serious disturbances occur in jails, the television sets are usually left intact, regardless of whatever else might be destroyed.

Radio should be dealt with in the same manner as television. Some of the newer facilities have jacks in the cells or dormitories that enable occupants to plug in earphones and listen to one, two, or three stations. This arrangement allows for the satisfaction of individual taste and a substantial reduction in the noise level in the institution. Some jails now permit inmates who will be confined for a comparatively long time to have their own radios. If this is to be the policy, it is suggested that radios must be purchased through the commissary. This ensures some measure of uniformity, eliminates the "You let his in, why did you keep mine out?" controversy, eliminates a way of introducing contraband, and cuts down on the possibility of theft or damage. Small transistor radios are recommended. Upon purchase, some sort of inmate identification should be soldered or engraved on the radio to reduce the possibility of theft.

Active Recreation

If the jail has sufficient provision for outdoor recreation, frequent use should be made of it. If there is no effort to provide organized activities, the boredom of the cellblock is just transferred to another setting. Basketball, softball, volleyball, shuffleboard, weight-lifting, among many others, are good activities. Additional use of the recreation yard can relieve the troublesome boredom that inevitably comes with a rigid routine. Weather permitting, some jails hold cookouts (hot dogs, hamburgers, watermelons, etc.) in the yard on holidays like July 4th and combine these with a schedule of field events such as races and basketball games.

Other Activities

If the facility does not have any outdoor recreation area, some part of the building should be identified and used for physical recreation. Weights, calisthenics, and other means of "working out" do not require vast areas and space. Minigyms are available at reasonable cost, require limited space, and provide opportunity for a variety of forms of exercise.

Table Games and Hobbies

Frequently, the recreational needs of inmates not interested in sports are neglected. Provision for a wide variety of other activities should be made.

Chess, checkers, dominoes, playing cards, and other table games are inexpensive and of interest to many people. In the past, there has been objection that such games might lead to gambling, but this has not proved to be a major problem. Inmates who want to gamble will find a way to do so; an alert staff can ordinarily keep it at a minimum so that gambling debts do not pile up. Crafts, such as leather working or painting, can provide many hours of wholesome activity at little cost. Some jails have solicited donations of musical instruments as another way of providing for a leisure time outlet.

Recreation Resources

A number of resources are available to help in developing and administering a recreation program. One of the best—and probably the most frequently overlooked—is the jail staff. Many staff members are quite proficient in a wide variety of leisure time activities (bridge, photography, etc.) and would be willing to share their knowledge and skills with the inmates. Someone who is a "bug" about a certain hobby enjoys nothing more than telling and showing other people about it. Use of this resource on either an assigned or volunteer basis usually makes an employee feel that he is more involved with the program and, justifiably, that he is making a significant contribution to the overall jail program.

Recreation presents a perfect opportunity to enlist active inmate participation in programmatic design and implementation. Left to the devices of even the most well-intentioned staff, the program will in all probability reflect staff taste in recreation, which is often substantially different from that of the population. An inmate committee could be chosen by the population for this purpose and meet regularly with the jail administrator or designated staff member. Such matters as determining which programs will be seen on the jail's televisions (either a precise schedule is prearranged and announced or frequent arguments result), planning special events and activities on holidays, deciding within budgetary constraints on equipment purchases, etc. are all appropriate for committee-staff review and consensus. Such an approach results in a more enjoyable and satisfactory recreation program, fosters mutual cooperation between inmates and employees that hopefully will extend into other operational areas, encourages the exercise of self-responsibility, and, for the committee members, provides a valuable learning experience. Parenthetically, where this committee approach has been tried, breakage and other damage to recreational supplies and equipment has declined markedly.

Other resources in this program area include the local department of recreation, the recreation department at an area college or university, or the local school district. The National Recreation and Parks Association is showing increasing interest in recreation in corrections, and their local chapter may be of considerable assistance. In addition, service clubs may be helpful in obtaining recreational materials. Musical groups and other entertainers will often agree to come into the jail and perform free of charge.

While access to recreation and leisure services should be readily available to all inmates, it is also possible to use recreation as an incentive. For example, one very overcrowded jail with little program space borrows movies (short subjects) on a wide variety of subjects and shows them three times a week to the dormitory that is the cleanest during inspection. Both inmate morale and jail sanitation have improved noticeably since the program began.

With proper use of both inhouse and community resources and a healthy bit of creativity, a good recreation program can be developed despite what may be inadequate physical plant provisions for recreation.

The Library

Both education and recreation are provided by a library. Hence every jail should have one. Reading material should take into account the varying interests of the inmates and should include educational material, magazines, fiction and nonfiction, standard reference works, and legal materials. Inmates should have regular access to the library and be able to borrow books from it.

Some jails find that permitting regular visits to the library weakens security coverage or causes other problems. If that is the case, arrangements should be made for an institution "bookmobile" or cart that circulates in the housing units regularly and thus gives inmates regular access to reading materials.

Selection of Reading Material

Two major areas of controversy arise when discussing library services in jail. The first is the access to legal materials and, specifically, what legal materials must be provided. All inmates should be given free access, upon request, to legal reference works regardless of their security classification or disciplinary status within the institution. Such access is a constitutional right and not a gratuitous privilege. Every jail should have available copies of the United States Code (annotated), the rules of federal court procedure, similar volumes pertaining to the jurisdiction in which the person is confined, and a good legal dictionary. Other volumes may also be appropriate, but the preceding constitute the minimal essentials of an inmate legal library. The inmates should also be provided with the means and facilities for the preparation of legal documents and materials—in practice, this can be a separate area of the institutional library, equipped with legal-size paper, a typewriter, and similar articles.

The second problem is censorship—what should and should not be allowed in the library as acceptable reading material. This area is also coming under the close scrutiny of the courts. Often, much staff time is used in deciding what is and is not proper reading material—time that could be better used on some other necessary jail function. Obviously books like *Escape from Jail Made Easy* pose a definite threat to the orderly administration of the jail, and such material should not be on jail library shelves. But, unfortunately, not all such decisions are that simple. A relatively easy rule of thumb is that whatever books could be taken out of or obtained through the local public library should be permitted in the jail library. Thus the jail is out of the censorship business, is using an objective criterion for its decisionmaking, and is treating its population like members of the community (which they are, especially those held in a pretrial detention status).

Staffing the Library

If possible, the jail should have either a full- or part-time librarian. This individual can catalogue the books, maintain supervision in the library, assist inmates with their reading needs, teach them how to make use of the resources of the library, and perform similar tasks. Failing a qualified employee for this position, use can be made of volunteers from the community, the services of a library science department at a local college or university, or the good auspices of the local public library. Certainly the local library can provide substantial assistance in properly setting up a well-rounded collection to meet jail needs. The special needs of those who do not read English should be remembered.

The Budget for the Library

Virtually every jail has a budgetary problem when it comes to purchasing sufficient books and periodicals for the library. There are several ways to overcome this problem. The local public library might be willing to establish a branch in the jail or provide regular bookmobile service. Area high schools and colleges might be able to donate some books.

Paperbacks not sold within a certain period of time are removed by newsstands or drugstores, the front covers are torn off, and the books are returned to the distributor. Frequently, local merchants are most willing to give these books to jails instead of returning them. Experience indicates that paperbacks are preferable for use in institutions because they require less space than hardbacks, are usually more current, and after several readings can be disposed of easily. It serves no useful purpose to decorate library shelving with old hardback books that are never read. Individual citizens, schools, and organizations can donate magazine subscriptions or hold book drives. These methods enable a jail administrator to add quickly to the reading material available in the jail and involve the community in improving the program. And they do not involve any expenditure.

Additional assistance in establishing or improving a jail library may be obtained from the state library and the Association of Hospital and Institution Libraries (a division of the American Library Association) in Chicago or one of its local affiliates.

Religion

The right to worship and practice the religion of one's choice is one of the constitutional rights of any United States citizen and one that has received strong reinforcement by court decisions concerning jail inmates. While an inmate cannot be forced to attend religious activities, he or she must be afforded the opportunity to worship if he or she chooses to do so. The availability of religious services in jails can do much toward fulfilling a basic human need, instruct individuals in a moral code and way of life that can be of substantial impact upon release, and, in a positive way, maintain a healthy tie with the community.

Components of Religious Programs

Religious programs in jails have several components. The most obvious one is providing regular religious services for the inmate populations. While it is impossible for most jail administrators to provide facilities for every denomination represented in a population, a Catholic mass and a Protestant service can usually be held each week. A synagogue will usually be glad to have a rabbi visit the jail and conduct services on the appropriate religious holidays. Members of the community will often make arrangements for the provision of special food. Many jails were constructed without chapels, so services are held in a variety of places within institutions—auditoriums, libraries, or dining rooms. The availability and schedule of services should be made known to the inmate populations. Ordinarily, local churches will provide part-time chaplains free of charge.

Pastoral Counseling

Another important part of a religious program in a jail is pastoral or spiritual counseling. A recognized member of the clergy should be available at the institution to provide religious instruction and counseling to those who desire it. Frequently, incarceration poses a crisis in the life of an inmate in which a chaplain can be of significant assistance. The chaplain may also provide counseling on an individual's family problems and other troubles of a nature that any pastor would deal with in a congregation in the free world. When a death, serious injury, or illness occurs, the chaplain can be of enormous help in notifying the family or, if the tragedy is in the family, the inmate.

The chaplain can provide major help in maintaining legitimate ties with the community and assisting in release preparation. The chaplain can maintain contact with the individual's family, employer, and other people who are important in the life of the offender. Frequently, the chaplain will be able to assist either the jail staff or the inmate directly in locating employment, temporary housing, or other necessary assistance in preparation for release. Members of the clergy are very much aware of community resources and are in a position to utilize them.

Resources for Religious Programs

Some jails have a position for a full- or part-time chaplain in their budgets. For those which do not, a phone call to the local Council of Churches, the office of the Catholic diocese, or similar bodies usually produces surprisingly quick results.

Organizations such as the Salvation Army and Volunteers of America also are willing and able to provide a wide range of services. These groups have considerable experience working in institutions and are quite understanding of and cooperative with the operating policies of jails. Local members of the clergy can also obtain the services of various volunteer groups in local churches, if such services are considered desirable.

Work and Activities

Most jail managers agree that a most serious problem in jails and the most difficult to deal with is inmate idleness. Archaic physical plants, lack of space, lack of personnel, and lack of funds all contribute to the problem. Again, an imaginative use of community resources may be the most promising solution to this dilemma.

It is well established that unsentenced prisoners may not be required to work, although the opportunity to work should be made available to them. It is to be hoped, however, that sentenced prisoners will have opportunities for work, training, and other programs for self-improvement. It is useless to create make-work projects merely to combat idleness, since such projects require a great deal of supervisory manpower and create needless disciplinary problems while achieving nothing in service to the jail or the community. Yet imaginative administrators have been able to provide purposeful work programs for inmates.

Types of Work Activities

The major area of concentration has, of course, been maintenance and operation of the jail itself—cleaning, painting, and minor repairs, as well as food service work. Furniture repair and maintenance, vehicle servicing and repair, duplicating services, and building and grounds maintenance may be provided to the jail and expanded to other county agencies. Such programs may be limited by the need for supervision, although departments receiving service may be able to provide staff who with some training can supervise inmate workers.

There are also numerous community projects with which inmates may help. These include stuffing envelopes for community fund and similar drives, recording books for the blind, and typing braille books. Another project that has considerable appeal is repair of donated toys for Christmas. Local firefighters and Marine Corps Reserve units frequently sponsor such programs. These groups collect the toys and provide paint and other materials as well as tools and supervision.

Training Values

Many of the preceding work opportunities have some training or skill-retention value. Because of the short time most individuals spend in a jail, acquiring a skill is unlikely; but there is the opportunity to test one's aptitude and liking for some kind of work, such as food service, painting, clerical work, or vehicle maintenance. This experience may be useful as a prelude to training release (fully discussed in Chapter 7) or postrelease training arranged by staff.

Skill retention consists primarily of permitting individuals to perform work at which they are already skilled in order to keep their skills, as opposed to acquiring new ones.

Issues to be Faced

Work activities should be extremely well planned to deal with such issues as:

How to provide vocational training as a basic entry to the work program. For example, in support of an automotive service and repair shop, an automotive repair vocational class may be set up in conjunction with a local high school. The U.S. Department of Labor has funds to assist in these programs.

How to charge the service clients for the work performed. Jail work, such as the previously mentioned automotive service and repair, that serves the sheriff's department or other local public agency should be offered at a reasonable charge. From this income, the inmate workers should be compensated under a predetermined pay schedule.

How to develop jail work projects in cooperation with local business and labor interests to assure that these projects do not constitute unfair competition. One example may be in the area of food service. Food service operations are not only a specialized skill but an important job market. It is now very common to find college and hospital cafeterias operated by contract. It should be possible to contract with a food service chain to operate the jail cafeteria and to employ as many prisoners as it can use. The prisoners would, of course, be employed on a work release basis, which requires prevailing wages less the standard deductions.

How to link assignments to jail work projects and performance thereon to the work release or general release and follow-up programs.

It is appropriate here to mention duties that inmates should not be permitted to perform. Under no circumstances should inmates be permitted to have access to security keys or locking devices, nor should they have any access to personnel or inmate records or drugs.

Volunteers

Citizen interest in the correctional process has been apparent for many years and is on the increase today. There are two ways to look at volunteers. One is that whatever nice people offer in the way of service has to be accepted with a smile either for political reasons or to avoid hurting anyone's feelings. But with increasingly sophisticated advances in the concept and practice of volunteerism, the major emphasis is now on responsibility to inmates and to the agency. In other words, if the services offered by volunteers are unwanted or not needed, there should be no compulsion to accept. However, with the relatively small, even nonexistent, program budgets of many jails, volunteers can be used quite dramatically to start and/or sustain desirable programs. Indeed services by volunteers are often superior to anything comparable that may be purchased.

On the surface, then, volunteers appear to offer an economical way to get needed work done. Volunteers can be used most effectively in such program areas as education, recreation and leisure services, libraries, religious activities, specialized programs such as Alcoholics and Narcotics Anonymous, and numerous others. One jail located a retired grocery store owner who volunteered to run the inmate commissary. In another jail a woman's club runs a day care center during visiting hours. The potential uses for volunteers are almost endless.

Essentials of Effective Programs

While volunteers can be of substantial assistance, they are not the total solution to the problems plaguing jail administrators. And volunteer programs in themselves sometimes have serious problems, usually because they lack one or more of the four essential components: (1) recruitment, (2) selection, (3) training, or (4) supervision. Without these four elements, a volunteer program can become more of a hindrance than a help.

Recruitment and Selection. Recruitment can be accomplished in a number of ways. One is to establish contact with any one of the many service organizations in the community, explain the problem, and seek ways in which the organization can provide assistance. Recruitment can be most effectively accomplished through a sound public relations program. Rarely does a jail administrator give a talk to a local group that jail needs are not mentioned and some offer of assistance is not made in response. Stories in local newspapers often strike notes of interest in many potential volunteers, who may not realize that the jail wants and needs such assistance. The Jaycees (Junior Chamber of Commerce) are particularly active in corrections these days. They have started a number of very successful projects throughout the country and have even established a post on the national level to coordinate these activities. In many areas, Lions and Rotary clubs sponsor programs of direct service to prisoners in the jails and postrelease assistance in job finding and counseling. Retired people have a wealth of talents and experience upon which to draw. But the use of volunteers should fit in with the overall program design of the jail and contribute to the plans and goals the jail administrator has established.

Selection should be geared to the task the volunteers will be expected to handle. Screening of potential volunteers should be based on such criteria as character and dependability. While most applicants will be genuinely well-motivated, one must be on the watch for those with self-serving or odd-ball motives, such as the young woman who "liked to be around a lot of men." The right kind of volunteer will not object to careful screening and, in fact, will be thankful for it, since screening indicates the seriousness of the task to be performed and the legitimacy of the program. Occasionally, someone will be motivated by a talk or some similar occasion to offer to volunteer and regret the decision later. During the screening process, provide a number of "honorable exits" that enable people to screen themselves out without embarassment. One example of this would be to ask the potential volunteer to take home an application form to fill out and take the initiative in returning it. Such procedures do not discourage the volunteers who are really qualified and wanted. Quality, not quantity, should be the objective of volunteer recruitment and selection.

One subtle treatment value of the dedicated volunteer is that his or her very presence challenges the "everybody's got an angle" life philosophy that many inmates hold. The paid employee, no matter how helpful or service oriented, can never achieve this. Many inmates find it difficult to believe, or have ever experienced, someone expressing an active interest in them without a blatantly selfish motive. Thus the volunteer, without even a conscious realization of the fact, can be instrumental in effecting a positive increase in feelings of self-worth and the beginnings of an attitudinal change. In realization of this benefit of volunteerism, the jail should take pains to ensure that no individual volunteer receives media publicity (that is an "angle"). All recognition for volunteers should either be on a purely in-house or group basis. Hence, the "joiner," the publicity seeker, and any similar genre of volunteers should be screened out during the initial recruitment process.

Training and Supervision. Training for volunteers should recognize that this is the first time most of these people have ever been in or connected with a jail. Consequently, training should include an orientation to the jail—its rules and regulations, programs, plans, procedures, and organization. Some description of inmates is needed to overcome the standard stereotypes. A brief description of the process by which someone gets to jail is very helpful. Most citizens have formed their impression of the judicial process from watching "Perry Mason," not actual bail hearings, magistrates, and public defenders. This approach will resolve many of the natural anxieties associated with "going to jail" as a volunteer. It will help the volunteer to understand his or her role better and have a "feel" for what the jail and the staff are trying to accomplish. Training should, of course, also be directed at the accomplishment of the specific task for which the volunteer has been recruited.

Principal responsibility for the volunteer program should be assigned to one staff member, though assistance may be required if the program is large or complex. Many of the volunteer programs that have floundered or failed have done so because the admininstrator believed that the program would "run itself." With the added increase in program activities that volunteers afford and the number of people coming in for a few hours a week, confusion and resentment in the regular staff can quickly result unless someone on the staff is fully aware of all aspects of the volunteer program, coordinates it, and interprets it to other jail personnel.

One of the more sensitive assignments that can be given volunteers is that of counselor or sponsor for an individual defendant or offender. It is here that selection, training, and supervision are extremely important. In addition, with some exceptions that may be made for very experienced volunteers, the inmate "client" should be interviewed and his or her situation and needs assessed by a trained professional for the purpose of determining (1) whether the needs are such that a volunteer can be of assistance, (2) whether volunteer services can be effectively utilized, and (3) to define as precisely as possible what the principal focus of the volunteer should be (for example, job-finding, housing, or family problems).

It should be noted that some individuals see volunteer counseling as an opportunity to satisfy their own curiosity or other needs. Such people are unsuited for counseling because of their inability to develop and maintain a constructive, problem-focused relationship with an inmate.

To the degree possible, the inmate and/or his problem and the volunteer should be matched. A young, mild, apologetic inmate should be matched with a volunteer who is basically optimistic and will provide encouragement and support. By the same token, a client who is aggressive and manipulative may relate best to a firm individual who establishes clear expectations.

There should be a system of recording, and each volunteer should be required to post the time spent and the activity engaged in. Supervisory staff should be readily available for consultation and discussion as needed, and supervisory conferences should be scheduled periodically to keep lines of communication open. Failure to do so can result in problems reaching such proportions that volunteers are embarrassed to bring them up for discussion.

Volunteers and Public Relations

Some jail administrators like to recognize the efforts of loyal volunteers periodically, say once a year or once every six months. Some jails hold receptions or dinners with a speaker; others give volunteers certificates. These approaches reward the efforts of the volunteers and make them feel appreciated. Such an event or ceremony is also good public relations.

One side benefit to having a volunteer program is the bridge it forms between the jail and the community. A volunteer obviously is going to talk about his work at the jail, usually in terms quite sympathetic to the jail's operation. Such word-of-mouth public relations results in increased community understanding and acceptance of the jail and its program efforts. It can be of substantial assistance to the jail administrator who wants to start a new program or otherwise improve the facility.

It is clear that volunteers can be of substantial assistance to the jail in many ways. Basically, only lack of imagination on the administrator's part and severe practical restraints limit the areas of help. But volunteer efforts can only work effectively if proper planning has preceded the volunteer program and a proper structure involving recruitment, screening, training, and supervision has been established. It does not take many dedicated, talented people to help make considerable improvement in a jail if their efforts are properly coordinated.

7

Work, Training, and Study Release

It's just impossible and illogical that you take persons away from normal society and put them in an abnormal society and expect them to adjust to the community.

Bennett J. Cooper

The prison is part of the community and the prison and the community share the mutual responsibility to re-train the offender. Work release, treatment and training go hand-in-glove inside and outside the jail. Prison and community working together can reduce criminality by exposing offenders to the many ways of becoming positive and productive members of society.

John D. Case and James F. Henderson

Definition

Work Release is a community-oriented correctional program that enables offenders to hold regular jobs in the community during the day, returning to their institutions at night. *Training* or *study release* is fundamentally the same as work release, except that the offenders are furthering their vocational or academic educations.

Rationale

Work, training, and study release are attempts to effect gradual reintegration of offenders back into their communities. The traditional pattern of incarceration followed by abrupt and total release in practice compels inmates to make immediate adjustments and role reversals from highly authoritarian, artificial environments, in which they have virtually no opportunities to exercise any type of self-responsibility, to complete freedom in often complex and frequently changing communities. If incarceration is an indicator that an individual had problems of adjustment in the free world prior to involvement in some sort of criminality, then certainly the abnormal microsociety of a jail can only exacerbate rather than alleviate those difficulties. While in confinement the offender undergoes a process of "prisonization,"[1] i.e., learning how to adjust to the norms of incarceration, not those of a free society. In order for a positive and successful readjustment to the community to occur, a bridge must be forged from jail to freedom that will effect a gradual reacculturation of the individual.

Work, training, and study release afford offenders the chance to partake in normal, significant activities in the community, though still incarcerated. Hence, if any adjustment problems develop, they may be recognized and rectified hopefully without any harm done to the community or the offenders. Work release enables offenders to accumulate funds for the eventual day of release and to gain self-confidence in their ability to support themselves. In addition, it provides employment that may be continued after release. All of this is accomplished by the offender as a part-time free member of the community to which he or she will return and within the demand and reward structure of the real world. Training and study release offer similar advantages, while the offender is acquiring a variety of skills and knowledge necessary for successful reintegration.

History

Work release came into vogue in the United States during the decade of the mid-60s to mid-70s. In 1959 North Carolina began placing felons on work release status and, with the significant success of that experiment, other jurisdictions were encouraged to follow suit. While in 1967 only 24 states had some statutory provision for work release, today all but one state has enacted the requisite enabling legislation for the program. Approximately 1665 jails have work release programs today and the number is still growing.[2]

Although widespread use of work release in this country is a recent development, the concept itself is over a century old. It is generally conceded that Sir Walter Crofton and Sir Joshua Jebb "invented" work release during the period of 1850-1870 as part of an integrated approach to dealing with convicted offenders in Ireland. This "Irish system" had three distinct parts: first, a period of penal servitude, i.e., incarceration in a maximum security prison; second, the intermediate plan, which consisted of a transfer to a minimum security facility and work release; and third, release on parole.[3]

This system was seen as a means of establishing a continuum of services for offenders. Under this plan, individuals progressed from one phase to another on the basis of behavioral and attitudinal change, which was verified by the careful observations of staff at all stages of the correctional experience. The major lesson to be learned from a critical examination of the "Irish system" is the need for that crucial intermediate step between incarceration and release, i.e., work release and minimum security surroundings. Crofton and Jebb believed that this decompression period was vital to successful postrelease reintegration.

The "Irish system" became the subject of much interest in the United States, and in 1869, Gaylord Hubbell, a well known warden from New York State, was dispatched to study it. He gave a most favorable report of his observations at the first annual Congress of the American Prison Association (now the American Correctional Association) in 1870. The assembled delegates apparently became so enthusiastic about the concept of parole that they totally neglected the crucial intermediate step of work release. As a result of this assembly, parole was introduced in the United States, but no action was taken on work release.[4]

Eventually, work release began in Vermont in 1906,[5] but it was not until 1913 that Wisconsin passed the first law (the Huber law) that formally sanctioned this rehabilitation strategy. But even as late as the 1960s, Wisconsin's implementation of this enabling legislation was sporadic—some counties used it and others totally ignored it.[6] In 1959 and the early 1960s, North Carolina showed that the program could work successfully on a large-scale basis with felons as well as with misdemeanants. In 1965 Congress passed the Prisoner Rehabilitation Act, which authorized the Federal Bureau of Prisons and, by extension, the District of Columbia Department of Corrections to establish work release and furlough programs. By that time, work release had become legitimized as an acceptable correctional technique in America. In the past decade, work release programs have been established throughout the country for both misdemeanants in local jails and felons in state and federal prisons.

Advantages to the Community

In addition to the obvious assistance that work release provides to the program's participants, it also conveys many direct and indirect advantages to the community.

First, since the people in the program are now working (as opposed to the involuntary idleness of the cellblock), they have become taxpayers instead of tax-users, paying all applicable federal, state, and local taxes.

Second, people on work release are required to reimburse the jail for room and board, usually at a rate of $5 or less per day. Thus the jail is recouping part of the cost of incarceration. On an annual basis, the amount collected via these reimbursement payments can be quite substantial, depending, of course, on the actual size of the program.

Third, many programs require participants to send a certain percentage of their pay to their dependents as support. Hence, a number of families will leave the public assistance rolls, thus effecting a further savings of taxpayers' funds.

Fourth, people on work release can be housed in minimum security quarters, which are far less expensive to construct and maintain than the typical jail living unit.

Fifth, since work releasees are in the community during the day, there is a corollary reduction in the number of security personnel needed on the day shift (or, if the jail is understaffed, some officers can now be assigned elsewhere in the institution).

There are also a number of less obvious advantages relating to participants' contributions to the gross national product and similar technical economic points.

Unlike virtually every other correctional program, work release not only has substantial potential as a reintegration device, but it also makes immediate and significant economic sense—a point of no little importance when attempting to convince a community of the program's merits.[7]

Other Programmatic Considerations

One major fallacy to which jail administrators sometimes fall prey is that once work release has been established, there is no longer a need for other programs. "From our experience we conclude that work release must include treatment. There is a danger in the program if the sole end is to make money for the county. If this is the case, work release centers can become nothing more than government-sponsored flophouses."[8]

Furthermore, an extensive work release program is dependent upon a somewhat favorable economy, since it is obvious that no matter how positive employers' attitudes may be to the program, inmates will be among the last hired and first fired. If work release is *the* program in a jail, a downturn in the economy or outright recession will mean the creation of substantial idleness in the institution. Since jails are part of the governmental process, institution administrators must await the results of a time-consuming appropriations cycle to obtain funding for alternative programs to cope with the idleness *after* it has become a serious problem. Of course, in poor economic times, the chances of securing program funding for jails are even more questionable, since the tax base is reduced and agency competition for existing funds is heightened.

Just because an inmate is on work release does not mean that all of his or her needs for services have been resolved. For example, the individual may need counseling to deal with continuing family problems, or adult basic education leading to a high school equivalency diploma may still be an appropriate goal. In fact, work release participation can create additional service requirements for some people. The inmate may well need some sound guidance on personal financial management, for instance, or counseling on how to cope with job pressures without quitting or slugging the boss. Often, it is these types of situations which, if left unattended, can lead to serious problems. One of the primary advantages of work release is that the institution is still in the position to identify and provide help to inmates with such problems, as opposed to the person who has been released outright and develops such difficulties and has no ready recourse to which to turn for advice and/or assistance.

Since work release participants are, by definition, sufficiently trustworthy to be in the community with little or no supervision, necessary services may be provided by allowing the individual to obtain them through an appropriate community resource or agency, such as the local school system's adult basic education program or a community mental health center. If such an approach is not feasible, institutional rehabilitation staff might be scheduled to provide services on a part-time or as-needed basis. Qualified volunteers, of course, are yet another potential resource for meeting the treatment needs of work releasees.

Additional Staffing Requirements

Depending upon the size of the program, there is a need for a part- or full-time job developer or job placement officer. Since most inmates were either unemployed or marginally employed at the time of commitment, they will need help in securing jobs. Experience has demonstrated that there is definite advantage to having a jail staff member responsible for developing a continuing relationship with the business community and serving as the primary contact between employers and the institution. Some proved techniques the job developer may use to win employer confidence include:

Emphasizing the thorough screening of inmates preceding their placement in the work release program

Providing testimonials from other satisfied employers associated with the program

Encouraging contact between the employer and the work releasee prior to actual employment

Placing emphasis on how much is at stake for the inmates

Citing the program's demonstrable success record

Allaying an employer's fears about having to "babysit" the work releasee

In certain instances, recommending hiring a work releasee on a trial basis

Emphasizing that the jail staff is readily available at any time in case of an emergency[9]

In large work release programs there is also a need for a part- or full-time bookkeeper to handle inmate accounts and disbursements in order to ensure the total accuracy of the important financial function. The larger programs often can severely strain the existing, limited accounting capabilities of jails.

Housing

Under ideal circumstances, work releasees should be housed in either a community-based residence or a separate facility in proximity to the jail that has been specifically designed for this purpose. If jail officials can trust a person to be in the community for 8 to 10 hours a day on a virtually unsupervised basis, then surely that same person does not require maximum security surroundings the rest of the time. However, few jails or jurisdictions can afford totally separate housing arrangements and are compelled to operate the program out of the main institution itself.

Housing is a critical issue in these programs. Since the participants are leaving and returning to the jail each day, they are a potential source for the introduction of contraband. The experience of many program administrators has been that in the majority of cases in which work releasees have smuggled something into the institution, they have been responding to pressures from other inmates who are confined in the jail without direct access to the community. "Bring back some grass with you today or I'll bust your head in" has sometimes provided sufficient motivation for an otherwise reliable work releasee to try to bring contraband into the jail.

The solution to this problem is to house work release participants in a separate area of the jail where they have no interaction with other prisoners. Without contact, there is no opportunity for untoward pressures to be applied, and the possibility of "slipping" contraband to other inmates has been greatly reduced or entirely eliminated.

Other Security Considerations

There are two other key aspects of assuring appropriate levels of security when administering a work release program. When participants are housed in the jail itself (even if they are housed in their own area), several other steps are useful in reducing the possibility of contraband entering the facility. First, upon their return from work each evening, an officer should frisk each participant. Second, a number of jails have found it practical to set up a "change" room near the entrance utilized by the work releasees. This room is equipped with lockers, and upon reentering the jail at night, inmates change from their "street" or working clothes into jail-issue clothing, storing the former in a locker. The next work morning the procedure is reversed. In addition to further reducing the possibility of contraband smuggling, this procedure also prevents a jail inmate in a more stringent security status from obtaining civilian clothing by which to effect some sort of escape attempt.

Another key aspect of ensuring public safety and security is for periodic checks to be made at the work releasee's place of employment to ascertain that he or she is, in fact, at the appropriate place at the proper time. It has happened that someone on work release has quit a job without telling jail officials and has continued to leave the facility each day to engage in illegal activities. Occasional job site checks, made by someone in civilian attire (perhaps the job placement officer), can be done discreetly without any possible embarrassment to the inmate and at sufficient intervals that they do not pose a harassment or inconvenience to the employer.

Screening

The single, most important component of the management of any community-oriented program is screening. While a jail should have utmost concern for the rehabilitation of the people confined therein, there is still an overriding responsibility to ensure the safety and protection of the public. There should be no question that at no time should anyone be placed on work release if jail officials believe that there is a reasonable likelihood that the person will use the opportunity to commit crimes or otherwise pose a threat to public safety. Hence, a thorough screening process must be employed to select participants for the program.

In establishing a screening mechanism, several crucial questions should be asked about each potential work releasee. First, is the individual in any way a threat to the community or is he or she extremely likely to remain crime free? Second, is the person sufficiently trustworthy to return to the jail each night after work? This, of course, assumes that the inmate needs the work release program, which, in all but a very few cases, he or she does.

Some of the factors that should be considered in the screening process include:

Conduct while in jail

Whether or not there are any outstanding detainers (warrants) against the individual from other jurisdictions

Prior history of alcohol or narcotics abuse

Prior criminal record

Prior history of violent behavior

Community contacts and ties

The foregoing is by no means a comprehensive compendium of all appropriate screening factors. Nor should a negative behavioral pattern or lifestyle *prior* to incarceration necessarily eliminate someone from positive consideration, e.g., a drinking problem five years ago could well have been conquered. But it is important to compile as much objective information as possible upon which to reach a reasoned judgment that is simultaneously responsive to the safety and best interests of the community and the needs of the inmate. Input should also most definitely be obtained from those staff members in most frequent contact with the inmate, i.e., housing unit officer, work supervisor, counselor, etc. The insights and observations of the staff who see the individual daily in a variety of situations can provide the proper framework within which to interpret the objective data. A thorough screening process is in the best interests of the individual inmates, the jail, and the community; can serve as the basis for overcoming some initial public resistance to work release programs; and, in the long term, can sustain the integrity of the program itself. The screening procedure is usually performed by the classification committee, with the jail administrator having the authority to approve or reject its recommendations.

It should be noted that in a number of jurisdictions, the authorizing legislation for work release specifically allows the sentencing judge to directly place someone in the program. Since the judge sees an offender for only a few minutes at the time of sentencing, while the jail staff observes him or her 24 hours per day, research has shown that judicially ordered work release participants have a higher failure rate than those selected by the jail staff. Yet, unfortunately, the public presumes that anyone on work release has been put there by the jail administrator; consequently, no matter the source of the program placement, the jail gets blamed for the failures. In a few jurisdictions, the jail staff may recommend someone for work release, but actual placement must await the approval of the sentencing judge.

Rules and Regulations

Usually, upon acceptance into the program, the offender signs an agreement authorizing the jail to make certain deductions and disbursements from his or her take-home pay, e.g., reimbursement for room and board to the institution and a stipulated amount to be sent to his or her family for support. The remainder of the earnings, minus incidentals such as car fare to and from work, is deposited in an account and given to the person on the day of release.

Part of the agreement also states that the inmate understands and agrees to abide by the rules and regulations of the work release program. Failure to follow these proscriptions can result in a variety of disciplinary actions ranging from a reprimand to removal from the program. Some of the most common rules associated with work release include:

Go to and from work directly without making any other stops or visits, unless specifically authorized by an institutional official.

Refrain from the consumption of alcoholic beverages.

Refrain from the use of any narcotics, unless prescribed or approved by the jail physician.

Do not cash a pay check upon receipt, but bring it back to the jail. (This rule exists primarily to prevent a work releasee from possibly having a few drinks after work, feeling some money in his or her pocket, and deciding to have a little celebration or to take a sudden cross-country excursion.)

In case of any emergency, sudden change in work schedules, or development of a major problem, call the jail at once.

These rules and regulations are fundamentally just common sense and are designed to assure the protection of the offender and the institution. Obviously, the commission of any crime while on work release is subject to full prosecution in addition to the individual's removal from the program. Similarly, failure to return to the jail after work is considered an escape and is subject to the same penalties as if the person had blasted his way out from behind the jail wall with a revolver. No doubt for public relations purposes, many jails prefer to call work release escapees "absconders," although no such distinction is made in the law.

The work releasee should be given some type of identification (a signed copy of the work release agreement might well be sufficient for this purpose) that attests to the fact that he or she is an authorized participant in the program, contains the jail's telephone number in case of emergency, and is signed by an appropriate staff member. Such identification is helpful should the offender be involved in an accident or is stopped for questioning by a police officer who inquires, "Didn't I lock you up a few months ago?"[10]

Public Relations

Since work release is a community-oriented program, to be successful it is essential that the community be receptive and supportive of it. Especially in the early developmental stages of a program, much of the general public will be suspicious of the concept, conjuring up images of wanton, career criminals being turned loose to prey upon them. These suspicions can readily become powerful opposition unless concrete steps are taken to allay rumor with fact.

It is extremely difficult to launch a campaign to sell a new concept to the public before a program has actually been established and some results achieved. Hence, it is helpful in the beginning to identify the key constituencies whose support is essential to eventual programmatic success. In the case of work release, these constituencies are the business community, organized labor, and the appropriate law enforcement agencies. Prior to the actual commencement of a work release program, it is advisable to meet with representatives of each of these groups to fully explain the rationale and operational techniques of the program and to elicit active cooperation and support. The local judges should also be briefed in advance, since the program will have major impact upon the people whom they are sentencing.

Members of the business community are obviously important, since they are the potential employers with the job opportunities needed by the inmates. Hence, without their understanding and action, the program cannot hope to succeed. Public-sector employment opportunities are becoming increasingly more important, but the approach to securing them differs, since the jail is already a part of the governmental structure. Interagency cooperation is obtained more through subtle persuasion and tradeoffs than by formal public relations.

Representatives of organized labor also have control over job and apprenticeship opportunities. Moreover, labor is often suspicious of any program that seemingly could threaten the security of the working person. If such a threat is perceived, a flurry of effective political activity frequently follows. Therefore, it is vital to explain to organized labor that work releasees will not be undercutting the local labor market—by specific stipulation of the enabling legislation, offenders must receive prevailing wages for the work they perform (they cannot be hired at significantly lower wages, thereby throwing others out of work or forcing existing wage scales down), nor can work releasees be used as "scabs" to break strikes. These are usually the major concerns of labor; and once they are addressed, union representatives are frequently supportive of the work release concept and occasionally offer to provide some sort of employment assistance.

Law enforcement agencies are responsible for assuring public safety and hence are suspicious of any program that might at first glance appear to be dumping convicted offenders on the street with little or no supervision. These agencies, both outwardly and subtly, can have a significant impact on public opinion of criminal justice issues. Therefore, as a professional courtesy, and as an attempt to get the local police to observe the program in action before forming any firm judgments about it, it is beneficial to candidly discuss what is being planned as well as its methods of implementation. Just like the public, the police are often unaware of the controls built into the program, e.g., careful screening, checks made on the job, etc. that are specifically designed to avoid precisely those problems which concern the police most.

The support or at least lack of concerted opposition from these key constituencies can be most instrumental in gaining community acceptance for work release. After the program has commenced actual operation and once some degree of valid success has been achieved, periodic press releases, speeches before various clubs and civic groups, and similar standard public relations techniques can be utilized to further demonstrate and sell the merits of the program. Work release *can* be effectively sold to the public, since it is not only good rehabilitation practice but is also cost-effective and both directly and indirectly saves the taxpayer money.

Continuing public relations serves the purpose of furthering community support and cooperation and also builds a residual, positive image base for the program. The latter is especially important since eventually, no matter how careful the screening, no matter how competent the administration, the untoward incident is bound to occur. The incident may be a new crime, an escape, or freak event that temporarily focuses negative public attention upon the program. Unless key elements in the community understand, support, and can defend work release, and unless there is a residue of positive public image, there may be considerable pressure mounted to suspend or close the program. Even though not all untoward incidents become major local issues, inevitably some event will occur to trigger substantial press coverage or strike the nerve of a powerful community organization. It is at these times that the importance of effective public relations becomes manifest, but at these times it is also too late to try and establish it. The end goal of such efforts is to establish a community climate in which work release is viewed as a desirable activity and one that benefits the entire community, so that the bad incident will be viewed within a framework of overall success and not seen in isolation as mistakenly representative of the program as a whole.

Training and Study Release Considerations

The same basic operational and administrative considerations pertaining to work release also apply to training and study release. Obviously, instead of seeking jobs, the institution tries to develop vocational training and academic educational opportunities in the community. Since the offender/students are not earning wages, training and study release do not have some of the economic advantages inherent in work release. Nonetheless, they are just as effective as a reintegration strategy.

By utilizing training and educational opportunities in the community, the jail is avoiding costly and often ineffective duplication of existing resources. The offender is becoming gradually reacculturated to life in the free world via exposure to and association with it; demands in community programs are frequently more realistic than in an institution and equipment and instructional techniques more contemporary and relevant; and whatever certificate or diploma is obtained is more acceptable to a potential employer and does not carry the stigma of "obtained in jail" with it. The same general screening and security procedures used for work release are also found in a well-administered training and study release program.

Conclusions

Work, training, and study release are invaluable means of establishing a bridge between jails and their communities for the purpose of successfully reintegrating offenders. By making use of available community resources, these programs allow offenders to become gradually reacculturated to the localities to which they will return, while simultaneously acquiring the skills necessary for "making it" upon release. Significant advantages even accrue directly to the taxpayer from work release, since offenders pay taxes, reimburse the jails for room and board expenses, and begin to support their families again.

A careful and thorough screening process ensures the safety of the general public. This, in combination with a well-conceived public relations effort, can result in community acceptance of such programs initially by several identifiable key constituencies and later by the public as a whole.

While work, training, and study release are not *the* answer to all the rehabilitation needs of jail inmates, they are nonetheless highly useful and relevant tools for the correctional administrator and represent a feasible and enlightened alternative to traditional modes of dealing with incarcerated offenders.

8 The Legal Rights of Prisoners

You have no rights—only those I choose to give you.
Warden Responding to Inmate's Request in 1965.

Throughout the greater part of the history of corrections, the courts have not been a major source of direction to the correctional administrator. All the legal mandates were contained in legislation, and the courts' role was very limited. In the past few years, however, the situation has changed until today, many see the courts, especially the federal courts, as the major impetus and instrument for altering the conditions of confinement.
The Emerging Rights of the Confined

Background

Not very long ago in American jails, prisoners quite literally had no rights. True, there was some vague protection offered by the Eighth Amendment to the Constitution, which forbade "cruel and unusual punishment." Until as recently as 1962, however, even that had not been judicially applied to the states.[1] Along with the advent of successful litigation in such social areas as welfare, public housing, and education, the courts began to take a serious look at inmate complaints. Previously the judiciary had informally developed a "hands off" doctrine with regard to internal jail matters in recognition of the special conditions requisite therein for the maintenance of peace and order, on a good-will assumption of administrative competence, and perhaps also because of the inartful preparation of legal materials by "jailhouse lawyers" acting without benefit of counsel.

Within the past decade, however, the courts, especially federal courts, have been deluged with prisoner suits that have questioned virtually every conceivable condition of confinement and correctional policy and procedure. Such operational areas as disciplinary rules and punishments, access to institution-provided legal materials, visiting and correspondence, adequacy of medical care, access to religious reading matter and provisions for services, and grooming standards have all been subjected to thorough scrutiny by the courts, which, in many instances, have ordered marked improvements and/or substantial revision of traditional administrative practices. In fact, with the possible exception of the question of a prisoner's right to rehabilitation, one can think of no major aspect of jail management on which a major judicial decision has not been handed down within the past dozen years.

Many jail administrators have become paranoid in the face of the ever-mounting tide of litigation involving corrections. To some extent, this is in reaction to a radical change in judicial philosophy concerning jail operation, i.e., instead of the administrator being all-powerful and answering to no one, he or she is now subject to potentially thorough and sometimes harsh scrutiny by the courts. And, to some degree, courts in a number of jurisdictions have indeed changed the way in which jails have been operated for decades. Furthermore, the torrent of lawsuits can be embarrassing and preparation of a defense both time-consuming and annoying.

The courts in most instances, however, have done little more than attempt to achieve a delicate alternative that is somewhere between the former "hands off" policy and outright interference in the day-to-day administration of jails and other correctional institutions. The major issues now having been decided, one can foresee a slackening in judicial interest and action in litigation concerning correctional institutions. While a few major decisions lay ahead, one can assume that the litigation of the past decade has set the fundamental precedents by which jails will be adjudged in the courts for some time to come.

Fundamental Principles

In order to properly understand the meaning and implications of the recent flurry of court decisions, it is essential to recognize several fundamental principles that seem to underly contemporary judicial thinking in this area. While inmates, because of their incarceration, may lose some of their *statutory* rights, they do not forfeit their *inalienable* or *constitutional* rights as United States citizens. A number of states have passed and enforced legislation that either substantially delimits or denies certain acquired rights to people convicted of crimes (these restrictions, in most instances, apply to people convicted of felonies and serving sentences in prisons as opposed to jails). Such statutory rights might include: holding public office, obtaining a license to practice a particular profession or vocation, divorce (making conviction of a crime grounds for divorce), owning or possessing a firearm (currently against federal law for a convicted felon), and similar matters that are subject to legislative regulation and governance. However, an inmate never forfeits his or her basic rights under the Constitution. The courts recognize, however, that the need exists to abridge the full exercise of these rights in some particulars because of the unique nature of a correctional institution and the inherent requirement to take extraordinary means to ensure safety and order therein.

But—and this is an essential part of the new judicial dogma of corrections—such limitations of rights must be justifiable and reasonable, not arbitrary or capricious. Hence, while most United States citizens may take a stroll anywhere they please, it is reasonable for a jail to restrict movement by promulgating and enforcing rules prohibiting inmates from perambulating through the front gate or over the wall. Conversely, while it may be permissible to house a known escape risk in secure isolation under certain circumstances, once so secured, hanging that person with handcuffs from the top bars on the cell door serves no useful purpose and hence is not allowable practice.

The imposition of the "reasonable" requirement has served to shift the burden of proof in jail cases. Heretofore, the administrator's actions were presumed legitimate, and it was up to the inmate to prove that they were not. Today, that presumption is gone, and the warden or sheriff must be able to demonstrate the validity and need for the particular practice or policy under dispute.

Strategy for Preventing Adverse Verdicts

The simplest way for any jail administrator to avoid losing cases in court is to periodically review recent court decisions affecting correctional institutions in concert with a competent attorney and to subject the facility's existing policies and procedures to a candid comparison with these standards. If some jail practice is contrary to judicial mandate, then it should be changed *prior to* the commencement of legal action.

The best advice any attorney can give a client is: "If at all possible, stay out of court." In defending a suit, there is always the risk of judicial overreaction, which could result in the imposition of strictures that could conceivably hurt the warden's or sheriff's ability to properly administer the jail. Furthermore, even if the correctional administrator wins the case, substantial expenditures of time and money and some degree of adverse publicity have been incurred. Even after having gone through a policy analysis based upon review of court precedents, the possibility of an inmate or group of inmates bringing suit still exists, of course. But very few judges anywhere will be inclined to rule against an administrator who can cite legal precedents as the rationale underlying a particular practice. To a judge such a managerial approach is the epitome of "reasonable" conduct and justification.

One further consideration that should not be overlooked is that such a strategy should be employed because it is right; every jail manager should be concerned that he or she is fully observing and protecting the rights of offenders. There are a number of cases in which the relief asked is beyond the direct ability and authority of the jail manager to provide. If, for example, the county or city refuses to appropriate funds to hire a physician, despite numerous requests from the warden or sheriff to do so, the jail might well lose a case brought to remedy the lack of adequate medical care. In such a situation, however, a court order to obtain the services of a qualified doctor will compel the local unit of government to take appropriate action. While the jail administrator may have lost the battle, he or she has won the war and, through an inmate-initiated suit, secured a service for the jail that for all practical purposes could not be obtained via the normal administrative channels and procedures.

Unfortunately, too many jail managers get hung up on "winning" or "losing," while failing to keep the end goal of improving the resources of the jail in sight. It is also regrettable that so many wardens or sheriffs are parochial in the extreme, i.e., fail to keep abreast of judicial and correctional trends outside of their own immediate jurisdictions, relying instead on the "because we've always done it this way" school of bureaucratic administration to justify policies and procedures. Today, neither sound management principles nor the courts permit such rationalization. The best defense in court for the correctional administrator is to be able to demonstrate a dynamic style of management that takes into account legal precedents, contemporary penological standards, and a genuine concern for the rights and well-being of the offenders and staff within his or her sphere of authority. No judge with common sense and a lack of masochistic tendencies wants to run a jail. But these jurists want assurance that the person who does is using the power and authority inherent in the position wisely and responsibly. It does not seem to be asking too much of a jail administrator to take sufficient steps to permit a judge to feel comfortable in so finding.

What the Courts Say about Prisoners' Rights[2]

Discipline

This area of jail operation has probably been the subject of more litigation than any other. Every aspect of the disciplinary process—what constitutes a legitimate rule or regulation, promulgation and notice to inmates, process, right to appeal (if any), right to counsel (if any), and the nature and degree of punishment—has been thoroughly scrutinized by the courts. In effect, by ruling against any disciplinary system that basically consists of the unfettered discretion of institutional employees,[3] the courts have wedded the concepts of due process and protection from cruel and unusual punishment to create a more formalized and objective means of administering discipline in institutions. In so doing, no court has ruled that discipline per se is not valid in a jail setting, nor that conduct that would not be in violation of any legal, cultural, or moral code if done in the free world cannot be proscribed legitimately by institutional rules, given the particular need of the facility to take extraordinary steps to ensure the maintenance of order and safety therein.

The first requirement, therefore, of a disciplinary system is that the rules of a jail must exist in a definite form,[4] and that proscribed conduct be stated in concrete rather than vague terminology.[5] In addition, these rules must not only exist on paper, but must be those actually employed by institutional staff.[6]

Since the courts now invoke a due process standard in adjudging the validity of disciplinary procedures, such a standard and common sense require that the regulations governing inmate conduct be sufficiently promulgated that all concerned within the facility know what the code of expected conduct is. In other words, if failure to make one's bed by 8:00 a.m. is a disciplinary offense, the inmates must be given adequate notice of this rule for it to have validity and be legitimately enforceable. The facility's rules must be clearly posted.[7]

Another way to achieve adequate notice is by issuing a small handbook to all inmates upon commitment. This booklet (which should also be available in Spanish in jails in which appreciable numbers of Spanish-speaking inmates are confined) would contain a statement of the facility's rules and regulations and applicable punishments, an explanation of the disciplinary process, and other such useful information as visiting hours and regulations, meal times, sick-call hours, which staff member to contact for a particular problem, programs and other services available at the jail, etc. This approach satisfies any applicable court standard, gives the newly committed person a brief orientation to the facility, and answers the most frequently asked and more important questions asked by new inmates, thus imparting useful information to the inmates and saving considerable staff time in constantly answering the same queries. If an offender is illiterate, the same information should be conveyed by a staff member during the initial classification interview.

If an inmate commits a minor violation of institution rules, which would not result in the loss of any privileges or otherwise noticeably or potentially affect his or her status within the facility, due process procedures need not be applied.[8] For example, if an inmate were walking down a hall without his shirt-tail tucked in (a violation, perhaps, of a grooming standard to be neat at all times) and an officer called his attention to this fact, a full-blown process need not be initiated. One would hope that most matters would be of such a minor nature that they could be so simply resolved at the lower echelons of the chain of command. When a more serious violation occurs, however, a formal proceeding that contains many of the basic elements of due process, is mandatory. *Wolff* v. *McDonnell* clearly defined the rights of inmates during the course of the disciplinary process and also mandated certain procedures on the part of institutional officials.[9] Some of the more important parts of this major decision are:

The inmate has the right to a written statement of charges no less than 24 hours before any disciplinary committee hearing.

The inmate also has the right to a formal notification of hearing and to be given time to prepare a defense.

The inmate can call witnesses and present evidence, as long as by so doing security or "correctional goals" are not jeopardized.

There is, however, no right to confront one's accusers. Permitting an inmate to do so is wholly discretionary on the part of institutional officials.

The inmate has no right to counsel at the hearing.

The inmate is entitled to a written statement of the disciplinary committee's decision and of the rationale for that decision.

Although this case technically involved only prisons, the process required by it has been held specifically to apply to jails as well.[10]

Wolff v. *McDonnell* attempted to strike a balance between legitimate institutional needs and the constitutional rights of inmates. In so doing, however, the decision makes it clear that proper protection of inmates' rights does not mandate the introduction of the full panoply of formal court procedures during the course of the disciplinary process.

In 1976 the United States Supreme Court in *Baxter* v. *Palmigiano* reinforced and expanded upon the *Wolff* decision. It added the following guidelines to be applicable to disciplinary hearings:

While the inmate has the right to remain silent, the disciplinary committee may use such silence against him or her in arriving at a decision (the doctrine of adverse inference).

The accused inmate has no right to cross-examine witnesses.

If the alleged violation is one for which the prisoner could also be prosecuted, then he or she has the right to counsel at the disciplinary hearing. Otherwise, there exists no right to counsel.[11]

The courts have also extended the definition of what constitutes discipline in a jail. Any decision apparently that results in grevious loss of privileges or deleterious alteration of an inmate's status within the facility constitutes disciplinary action.[12] Thus, if an inmate were to be reclassified from medium to maximum security status with its attendant greater restrictions on personal movement, smaller range of possible job assignments, and fewer recreational opportunities, such reclassification action would have to be subject to a due process hearing conducted in much the same fashion as regards safeguards and rights of the inmate at a disciplinary hearing.

Methods of Punishment

The Eighth Amendment provides that people shall not be subjected to "cruel and unusual" punishments. The Supreme Court has made it quite clear that the definition of *cruel and unusual* is not absolute. In the Court's language, "The words of the Amendment are not precise, and . . . their scope is not static. The Amendment must draw its meaning from the evolving standards of decency that mark the progress of a maturing society."[13] In practical terms, this concept ". . . is not fastened to the obsolete but may acquire meaning as public opinion becomes enlightened by humane justice."[14] In other words, contemporary standards of human decency define what is considered "cruel and unusual." In the colonial era, branding was deemed an appropriate and acceptable punishment, while today it would be considered intolerable barbarism. Similarly, acceptable punishments today might well be the cause of shock and outrage to society 25 or 50 years hence.

Corporal punishment in all its forms is proscribed. " . . . [I]t is safe to affirm that punishments of torture . . . and all others in the same line of unnecessary cruelty, are forbidden."[15] A whole range of specific acts, such as lashing[16] or tear-gassing an inmate who is not presenting a physical threat[17] have been forbidden by the courts.

This prohibition against corporal punishment, however, does not rule out the use of force in legitimate circumstances, e.g., a guard involved in a fight with an inmate[18] or moving an inmate who has refused to go voluntarily with the least necessary force.[19]

Aside from the issue of corporal punishment, "there are generally three tests for determining whether a punishment is cruel and unusual."[20] "But punishments which are not *per se* cruel and unusual may become so if they are disproportionate to the offense committed."[21] "The other two [tests] are whether it is of such character as to shock the general conscience, and whether, although applied in a pursuit of a legitimate penal aim, it goes beyond that which is necessary to achieve that aim."[22]

Thus, as just one of many examples, placing an inmate in solitary confinement under incredibly primitive conditions for a substantial time period for failing to sign a piece of paper to the effect that he had read the safety rules in the shop in which he worked was found to be a disproportionate punishment.[23] Placing an inmate naked in an otherwise empty concrete solitary confinement cell; with no blanket; with a "toilet" (which consists of a hole in the floor) that cannot be flushed from inside the cell; depriving him of all hygenic items, e.g., soap, toilet paper, toothbrush and paste; and placing him on a restricted diet has been found to be treatment, in effect, shocking to contemporary societal standards.[24] Similarly, the old reliable bread and water diet has been ordered into obscurity by the courts.[25] In addition, courts will no longer condone measures far beyond those which are necessary to achieve a valid penal aim. For example, for purposes of ensuring the safety of staff and other inmates, a person may be segregated from the general population, but beyond that, denial of privileges must be justifiable within the framework of that need (doctrine of least restrictive alternatives).[26] Coincidentally, segregation for such purposes may be made without a hearing (which may be held subsequently within reasonable proximity to the actual event) under circumstances of actual or imminent violence.[27]

Exercise and Recreation

Inmates must be allowed the opportunity for outdoor exercise.[28] An hour per day has been established as a minimum standard,[29] although the same court later modified that to five one-hour exercise periods per week.[30]

Medical Care

An institution has an affirmative duty to provide medical care sufficient to meet the needs of its inmates.[31] In at least one instance, a federal judge ordered a jail to give all newly committed inmates a physical examination.[32] Such a standard, if compelled in other jurisdictions, would result in a noticeable improvement in jail health care services, but such a judicial trend has not yet been established widely on this point. Quite understandably, judges are reticent to second-guess the quality of medical services provided. As long as a particular course of treatment is "acceptable practice" within the medical profession, judges will normally accept it as adequate. In those instances in which an inmate disagrees with the course of treatment, the court will find in favor of the institution as long as such treatment meets the test of being "acceptable practice."[33] In one isolated case, a judge ruled that it was cruel and unusual punishment for a jail not to make provisions to continue inmates on methadone maintenance who had been participating in such a program at the time of commitment.[34]

Clothing and Attire

Other than the necessity for a jail to provide adequate clothing,[35] there has been comparatively little litigation on this subject. The major cases have involved the question of whether or not institutions must permit the wearing of religious medallions (if one religious group is so allowed, others must be given the same privilege on the grounds of freedom of religion[36] unless the medallion is of such a material or design as to constitute a threat to security[37]).

Grooming and Personal Hygiene

There have been a considerable number of inmate lawsuits challenging institutional regulations pertaining to haircuts, length of hair, and beards and moustaches. Most of these suits have been based upon a purported freedom of expression or right to privacy. Jail officials have countered that such rules are necessary for sanitary and security (i.e., identification) purposes. Since there have been so many cases on this matter, it is possible to find rulings that are supportive of either side. In general, however, such rules and their enforcement have been found to be valid when dealing with sentenced prisoners.[38] Unsentenced inmates apparently have the right to personal flexibility in hairstyles and whether or not to have a beard, as long as they meet common standards of personal hygiene, i.e., no lice or other vermin.[39] Furthermore, an inmate cannot be forced to have his hair cut contrary to his valid beliefs in a legitimate religion.[40] In addition jails must provide items of personal hygiene, such as toilet paper, to inmates without charge and daily.[41]

Miscellaneous "Environmental" Conditions

Jail officials must keep the facility in a reasonable state of cleanliness, since filthy conditions violate Eighth Amendment rights.[42] Plumbing must be adequate and leaks repaired.[43] Showers must be kept in working order, and washing and toilet facilities must be maintained in a sanitary condition.[44] Lack of adequate ventilation[45] and/or heating[46] violates the Eighth Amendment prohibition against cruel and unusual punishment.

Mail Censorship

This is one other area of institutional operation that has become the subject of much legal controversy in recent years. At one time, all incoming and outgoing mail was opened and read. Inmates were limited to sending and receiving letters only from those people on a restricted and formally approved correspondence list. Incarcerated people were obviously not permitted to use correspondence to foster escape attempts, but also could not criticize the jail or its officials, mention other inmates by name, or complain about conditions within the facility.

Today, a number of jails no longer read all mail, but do open it to check for contraband. Some institutions have also done away with the formality of a correspondence list. It should be noted, however, that censorship is still permitted by the courts,[47] and most jails still continue this practice in some form. Censorship is allowable because officials argue that it is necessary to maintain an appropriate degree of security. However, in meeting this valid objective, administrators are obligated to use the least drastic form of censorship, since any censorship is, in effect, a curtailment of First Amendment rights.[48] One recently decided case may indicate the start of a new trend in judicial decisions in this area. In *Gates* v. *Collier*[49] the court held that the reading of inmate mail is not permissible, although such correspondence may be opened and inspected for security reasons. Because of the privileged nature of the attorney-client relationship, letters to and from an inmate's attorney cannot be censored.[50]

Visiting

In examining visiting practices and procedures in jails, the courts generally recognize that some control, in the form of approved visiting lists, is necessary in order to maintain security in the facility because of the threat of the introduction of contraband and the possibility of escape attempts. Furthermore, the adequacy of the number and length of visits must be determined to some extent by the capacity of the physical facilities available for such purposes.

That inmates are entitled to visits is no longer in dispute. The major controversy at the moment relates to so-called contact visits, i.e., the inmate is allowed to hold or shake hands with the visitor and, in the case of a visiting spouse or boy or girl friend, kiss the visitor at the beginning and end of the visit. In *Oxendine* v. *Williams* the court held that no such right to contact visits existed.[51] In similar cases, however, in widely disparate areas of the country judges have ruled that jails must make provision for contact,[52] although limitations may be imposed depending on the classification status of the inmate.[53] This latter judicial course appears to be the one that will become predominant in such cases in the near future. While contact visits are required in some jurisdictions, there is no constitutional right to conjugal visitation.[54] Jail officials are within their rights to take appropriate means, such as searching any or all visitors,[55] to ensure institutional security. In analyzing the plethora of court decisions on visiting, the distinct impression is given that in the future, courts will tolerate fewer restrictions on visits and their conditions for unsentenced prisoners than for those who are serving a sentence.

Access to Legal Materials

In April 1977 the United States Supreme Court ruled in *Bounds* v. *Smith* that prisoners must be given access to law libraries.[56] If the institution does not choose to maintain a collection of standard legal reference materials, inmates must be afforded the opportunity to use them somewhere else, e.g., at a nearby institution that does have such a library. While this decision specifically impacted a state prison system (North Carolina), in effect, it also served to affirm a number of lower court rulings that had made similar findings in cases involving jails.[57] The rationale underlying these decisions is simply that it is a fundamental right of any American to have access to the courts, and this is especially true in instances in which the inmates involved are being detained prior to trial, inasmuch as they are still presumed innocent. As a 1966 federal court decision unequivocally stated, "A right of access to the courts is one of the rights a prisoner clearly retains. It is a precious right and its administrative unfettered exercise may be of incalculable importance to the protection of rights more precious."[58]

Jailhouse Lawyers

The jailhouse lawyer of cliché fame has also been officially legitimized by the Supreme Court. In *Johnson* v. *Avery*[59] the Court held that, in summary, "legal assistance to inmates by other inmates must not be prohibited by prison officials in the absence of a realistic and workable alternative program of legal assistance."[60] However, institutions may establish reasonable rules concerning the conditions (place, time, etc.) under which this assistance is provided within the framework of the following formula: "If the application of the [institution's] rule impedes or discourages mutual prisoner assistance to a significant degree, the burden of justification will be great. If, on the other hand, the application of the rule results in mere inconvenience to prisoners seeking legal assistance, and there is a clear institutional reason for the restriction, the rule must be sustained."[61] As a result, the main controversy on this topic now focuses on the legitimacy of specific, applicable jail rules and regulations.

The Right to Safety

Within the expanding framework of prisoners' recognized legal and human rights, perhaps none is more fundamental or important than that of safety. How can someone who has been the victim of an egregious assault while incarcerated fail to emerge from the jail experience embittered and vengeful? This is especially true in those instances in which the person was merely being detained pending trial and was eventually determined to be innocent. How can a young first offender concentrate on participation in a rehabilitation program if he is terrified by the very real prospect of mass homosexual rape on his return to the cellblock? This particular problem has become so bad that several courts have ruled that such fear, under certain circumstances and when documentably justifiable, can be an acceptable defense to a charge of escape.[62] When a person is convicted of a crime and incarcerated, no sane society would contend that assault, rape, stabbing, and even murder are consciously contemplated or acceptable methods of additional punishment. As a judge succinctly stated, "Government owes to those whom it has deprived of their liberty an even more fundamental constitutional duty to use ordinary care to protect their lives and safety while in prison."[63]

A jail official has the obligation to take reasonable steps to ensure the safety of inmates. The debate, therefore, centers around the definition of the term *reasonable*. Part of the current legal delineation of the meaning can be found in *Cohen* v. *United States*,[64] which held that a prison has the obligation to make a reasonable classification of a prisoner, and once made, "the government has a duty to take reasonable care in maintenance of his custody." In other words, given the facts in that case, the administration must try to determine which prisoner(s) poses a threat to institutional security, including to the safety of other inmates, and once that determination is made, to take the appropriate steps to maintain that person(s) in a fitting degree of custody.

In another pertinent case,[65] the entire Arkansas state prison system was held to be unconstitutional, in large part because of the astounding prevalence of assaults and homosexual attacks. Among the remedies mandated by the court were the initiation of a sound classification system and the provision of more adequate staff supervision. "It should be noted that the lack of proper classification of the inmates which resulted in young first offenders being housed with "hardened criminals" was one of the major deficiencies which influenced the final outcome of this case."[66] Similar findings have been made in other cases in which jails specifically were involved.[67]

Recently, inmates who have been victimized during a term of incarceration have been suing units of government, correctional institutions and agencies, and administrators for damages. These suits have been brought as negligence actions, alleging a tort liability on the part of jail officials (failure to adequately perform certain basic, required duties) or under one of several federal civil rights acts. This development is a new twist in jail litigation, since heretofore most suits merely sought the alleviation of certain conditions of confinement.

This recent trend has been hampered somewhat by the legal doctrine of "sovereign immunity" that still prevails in 12 states. Simply stated, *sovereign immunity* means that "any suit against an officer or agent of the state, in his official capacity, in which a judgment can be rendered controlling the action or property of the state in a manner not prescribed by statute, is a suit against the state and cannot be maintained."[68] The problems caused by this doctrine, where it exists, have resulted in plaintiffs' attorneys resorting to the use of civil rights legislation in order to gain valid standing to institute lawsuits.

The approach of the courts in these cases to date gives some clue as to what is and will be determined "reasonable" action to maintain inmate safety. Frequently, a key to the outcome of the case is the testimony of an expert penologist, whose opinion is sought regarding the validity of the jail official's actions or omissions based on penological standards and/or prevailing practices in the field. This raises questions concerning classification, adequacy of staff supervision, numerical adequacy of staff, supervision, training and qualifications of staff, management practices of the jail, including close scrutiny of operational policies, practices, and procedures, among others.

In practical terms, in an assault case, for example, were the assailant and victim properly classified? Were institutional policies adequate relative to maintenance of appropriate levels of custody? Was staff made aware of these policies, adequately trained in their implementation, and were, in fact, the policies properly carried out? If a weapon was used, where did it come from? Were adequate preventative measures in force and taken to prevent inmates from obtaining weapons (such measures include regular shakedowns, frisks, standard methods of controlling inmate movement, etc.)? These and other similar types of questions concerning all aspects of policy and operation relating to the incident must be asked. If the jail official's actions are reasonable in light of acceptable penological standards, the incident might not have been feasibly preventable—violence can occur in a jail that is very well managed and has sufficient, capable, and competent staff. But if policies and procedures do not reflect a commonly accepted definition of sound jail management, or supervision of staff is poor, or a staff member failed to follow procedures, etc., a finding of negligence and damages may result.

In one recent case, a man on his second day in jail (charges were subsequently dropped) was stabbed so viciously that the attack resulted in a permanent disability, thereby severely limiting his potential to provide for his family.[69] The assailant, a maximum security prisoner, had somehow obtained a butter knife, gone through nine locked doors (each of which had to be opened by a guard), committed the stabbing (which was facilitated by a guard's unwitting failure to lock a cell door according to established procedure), and then returned through those nine doors carrying a bloody towel and, for a part of the way, leaving bloody footprints. During the trial, several other points pertaining to possible negligence were also raised. The jury awarded the victim a judgment of $597,500.

In a rape case, a young man was awarded $50,000 by a jury when it was shown that the absence of a classification system, poor managerial practices, and poor supervision of staff had a causal connection to the attack.[70] Despite the judgment and the attention it created, an almost identical incident subsequently occurred in the same jail, and that victim is likewise bringing suit.

What these and similar cases are saying is that jail officials have a legal obligation to safeguard inmates and that failing to take reasonable steps to do so, inmates are liable to sizable awards for damages. Previously, an inmate might have been able to petition a court to obtain a change in jail conditions to prevent a recurrence of an act, but now can recover directly for the injuries sustained. This development will probably stir an increased awareness on the part of inmates of their rights. One would also assume, though not necessarily correctly, that the jail officials faced with this negative alternative to proper jail management will take steps to effect a marked improvement in day-to-day institutional operations by referring to and then applying applicable penological principles and standards. Inmate protests can be controlled; the efforts of concerned citizens might be diffused through the maze of bureaucracy; temporary political pressure might successfully be "stonewalled," but a hefty court judgment is rather difficult to ignore. If this current trend is any indication, some type of noticeable improvement or reform will have to take place, unless units of governments and individual jail managers are willing to pay out sizable sums in damage awards as the price for continuing to do business as usual. The irony is that in many of these cases, it would not have taken sizable expenditures to improve conditions in order to prevent these incidents. Adequate resources were there already! They just were not organized and supervised properly by any standard of decent management, which is probably the most incredible observation to result from a close analysis of these cases.

Staff Rights

The recent explosion of cases delineating, expounding, and expanding inmate rights has served to create a seeming paranoia on the part of many administrators and staff members, who are now wondering if they have any rights. This concern has become so pressing that the American Correctional Association has recently issued a publication on the subject.[71] With the seemingly radical change in disciplinary procedures imposed by the courts came the complaint that "they don't want us to enforce discipline any more." Concurrently, administrators were accused of letting "the inmates run the joint."[72] These reactions, in turn, led to a serious morale problem in institutions.

In effect, jail administrators and staff have the same rights they have always enjoyed (including the right of a guard to sue a warden or sheriff for negligence). What has been curtailed is the degree of discretion that may be exercised in fulfilling the duties of the position and expressing those rights. Heretofore, virtually no actions of jailers were subject to review outside the institution. The only limits imposed upon discretion were those promulgated by the administration. What the courts are saying, in effect, is that absolute discretion does not afford sufficient guarantees of the legitimate rights of inmates. Hence, objective procedures, policies, and systems must be developed as a protection against the possible abuse of authority. With adherence to these guidelines, an employee is free to take whatever reasonable actions are necessary to successfully fufill his or her duties and responsibilities.

The balance being struck by the courts is between "reasonable" and "necessary," on the one hand, and "arbitrary" and "unfettered" use of discretion, on the other—*not* between inmate versus staff rights. The moderation of power inherent in such judicial decisions is in such marked contrast to traditional jail practices and has developed so rapidly in so many legal areas that its intent and effects have been misperceived by both administrators and staffs. While some of the court rulings may have resulted in inconvenience or added complexity to certain jail practices, they have not sought to prohibit staff from achieving legitimate penological goals through the exercise of reasonable means. In other words, instead of just "doing it," the jailer must now be prepared to justify his or her action(s)—a significant change in traditional jail administration that some officials find a very difficult adjustment to make. The existence now of a substantial body of case law affecting jails has no doubt added to the complexity of an already difficult job, necessitating that an added element be considered in managerial decisionmaking. However, these decisions have not abrogated, nor have attempted to abrogate, the rights of management and staff, nor have they posed an insurmountable obstacle to the achievement of the fundamental missions of a correctional institution.

The Next Battle

In reaction to substantial changes in the operation of some jails and the perception that management is more concerned with prisoners' rights than with the staff's, many jail employees, in an obvious desire to obtain higher wages and better working conditions, like many other public-sector employee groups, have in the last few years been increasingly represented by unions.[73] In a number of jurisdictions, not unlike other public employee unions, these labor groups are becoming more militant. Organized and wildcat strikes, "sick outs," and similar activities have attracted wide attention and have caused increasing concern to administrators.

Since in most places salaries are established by a legislative body, contract negotiations with administrators focus on work conditions. In jails, these conditions are greatly influenced by operational policies and procedures, and many unions are now trying to have a greater voice in the creation or alteration of these procedures. In so doing, there may well be conflicts between the demands of the employee's union (and the eventual content of their negotiated contract) and some of the inmate rights previously discussed. Such a conflict would place a jail manager in a most unenviable position, with substantial and competing pressures converging upon him or her. This could well result in some complex and intense battles in court that would clarify in greater detail than has been done before the mutual and respective rights and responsibilities of staff and inmates in relationship to each other. In such a scenario, caught between his or her two most important constituencies, it is difficult to foresee how a jail manager could win, given the undesirable institutional climate that might well be a distinct side effect of such litigation. The jail official who has diligently mastered the law of prisoners' rights must now be prepared to learn the labor law of correctional administration. "Every time I learn the rules, somebody changes the game."[74]

Summary

Within the past decade, the courts have abandoned their previous "hands off" doctrine in regard to the question of prisoners' rights and have sought to thoroughly delineate them and, further, to ensure them by placing parameters on the heretofore unbridled discretionary power of jail officials. In so doing, jurists have established and/or reinforced several fundamental principles relating to the prisoner as a person and citizen who, despite his or her special status while in confinement, is nonetheless guaranteed the protections afforded by the Constitution. By their rulings judges have compelled changes in various aspects of traditional jail operation, most notably in disciplinary procedures and methods of punishment. Virtually every particular of incarceration has been subjected to piercing judicial scrutiny.

With the volume and variety of cases already decided, few essential legal questions remain to be answered. While litigation will, of course, continue, sufficient principles and precedents have been established to enable the administrator (and his or her legal advisor) to perceive which policies and practices will be considered legitimate and which will be censured by the courts. One key issue, however, that has yet to be decided is whether or not an inmate has a right to rehabilitation—a point not without significant and substantial ramifications.

A relatively new and, to jail administrators, potentially threatening type of litigant is the inmate who has been victimized while incarcerated and brings a damage suit for the alleged negligence. In effect, the inmate is now not just entitled to certain fundamental rights but, particularly as regards his right to safety, can recover damage awards for the violation of those rights if the jail has failed to properly discharge its responsibilities. Several recent cases in this area of the law amply demonstrate just how far the courts have gone in reversing the "hands off" doctrine.

Many jail officials feel that the courts have extended prisoners' rights too far, thereby hampering them in the administration of their institutions. Rather, what judges have done (or at least attempted to do) is to strike a balance between legitimate inmates' rights and the valid interests and obligations of the government and jail administrator. Instead of virtually unreviewable management by fiat, jail wardens or sheriffs must now be prepared to justify actions as "reasonable." The courts have not prohibited discretion on the part of administrators and staffs, but rather have attempted to halt the arbitrary use of power without sufficiently valid purpose and at too great a compromise of fundamental, guaranteed rights. The courts, in effect, have ordered change, which is never easy for any bureaucratic institution to accept.

In response to the courts' concern for inmates' rights and other internal changes within the jail field, corrections personnel have become increasingly concerned with staff rights. In combination with other factors, such as the rise of unionization in public-sector employment generally, this has led to the rapidly increasing organization of line jail employees. This development is already having some impact on yet another area of jail management. It also bodes for a potential conflict (with serious potential repercussions) between jail reform and innovation, prisoners' rights, and the rights of employees, especially as enunciated in union contracts.

This chapter does not pretend to have presented a comprehensive compendium of prisoners' rights, nor of all the court decisions pertaining to them. Access to media, work assignments, grievances, and detainers are just some of the areas that have been omitted in which there have also been a significant volume of cases and new precedents established in recent years. What this chapter has attempted to do is to outline significant developments in some of the major areas of interest, to identify judicial trends, and to delineate the essential principles underlying the courts' approach to the entire question of prisoners' rights. If these goals have been accomplished, then you will have obtained a basic feel for the topic and be able to gauge specific jail practices by the fundamental guidelines utilized by the courts. The cases cited herein were selected on the basis of relevancy, or recency, and/or as preeminent precedents on particular points. It should be noted, however, that due to the tremendous volume of cases concerning jails, relevant decisions are being handed down by the courts continually and some of these may well amend or change some of the specific conclusions drawn in individual sections in this chapter.

The whole issue of prisoners' rights is obviously highly complex and wrought with ramifications of a most important nature. In essence, judicial actions as a whole over the past decade have contained a clear message for jail managers: Inmate rights must be recognized, understood, and, as much as is possible within the unique mission of a jail, protected by administration and staff. Many jail officials have always done that. But the abuse of discretionary power is what is brought to the attention of the court and becomes the basis of judicial action. Viewed from that perspective, the rulings of the past decade are not a condemnation of jail officials per se. However, these cases do serve to establish necessary guidelines upon which the competent warden or sheriff may base his actions with confidence, and they provide inmates with a legitimate recourse when their rights are abridged by the abuse of legitimate administrative authority. Because of its newness, the balance is perhaps somewhat tenuous and confusing at this time; but nonetheless, it is one that will eventually serve to protect the interests of all parties within the jail community—administrators, staff and inmates.

9

The Jail's Role in Community Corrections

*We don't want those over-the-mountain people [from the state capital]
coming in here, telling us what to do, and dumping their problems on us.*
Community Leader

Introduction

Many people exhibit a near paranoia about any direct state or federal intrusion into their communities. The occasion for the preceding expression of suspicion and disdain for state government was the pending expiration of an arrangement under which the state and county had jointly established a model work release center in a city on Colorado's "Western Slope". The program itself had experienced a phenomenal (and verified) success rate. The question under discussion was whether the state should assume total fiscal responsibility (and, thus concurrently, all operational authority) for the program in the future or whether the county was willing or could afford to take over the program on its own. The conclusion reached in meetings with various civic officials was devastatingly direct, i.e., unless the community can somehow take over the program entirely, the work release center should cease operating. "We lived happily in this community before the program and we can live happily without it, if need be, in the future" was the blunt summation given by one decisionmaker.

In essence, the main arguments against state control were quite simple, even if, on an objective basis, they are somewhat open to debate. The state was experiencing some major problems and, even more to the point, in the more removed areas of Colorado, Denver was gaining the reputation of having acquired many of the serious ills seemingly a part of major metropolitan areas throughout the country. If the state government had one way or another messed up Denver as much as it had, then other communities would be damned if the bureaucrats would ruin their placid lifestyles and, in the case of corrections, start dumping problem inmates from the Denver area onto them. Whether any or all of these perceptions were valid is quite immaterial. The key point is that the local people adamantly believed them to be the truth and had girded to do battle with the "over-the-mountain people," if necessary, to protect their community. This little drama occurred in 1976 and is a classic example of American independence coming to the fore against the threat of big government interference in daily life.[1]

Although the locale involved could be understatedly called a conservative area, surprisingly the people are quite supportive of community-based alternatives to traditional incarceration. But they are only willing to deal with their offenders, not with those from other areas. The key element in the success of the existing work release center was that it was run by an individual who had lived in the town for many years and had consummate credibility with virtually everyone who lived there. This man was known, respected, and trusted locally, and as long as he was in charge of things, local interests would be protected. When it was subtly pointed out that the center had, in fact, served offenders from other areas of the state, the attitude seemed to be "Well, he must have his reasons" and the practice, if not joyously accepted, was passively tolerated.

The Jail as a Local Institution

The reason for relating the foregoing saga is to illustrate the actual attitudes of one community toward local versus state control and operation of programs. Interestingly, there was no controversy surrounding the idea of work release per se in this small city not prone to massive expressions of liberality on social issues. The entire basis for contention was fundamentally a substantial distrust of policymakers who did not have a direct, personal stake in the life of the town. Regardless of the source of the funds (and certainly no one objected to outsiders paying the bills), local control meant security and integrity of the program; state control was equated with the worst nightmares of the most virulent espousers of the law and order doctrine.

One of the few advantages that the jail has in the correctional milieu is that it is the quintessential local institution. While in many jurisdictions probation is also administered locally, few people really understand its function (or that it is, in fact, different from parole) and this confusion is compounded by its close relationship to the courts operationally and, in numerous instances, administratively as well. Prisons are places to which local troublemakers are exiled at the expense of the state, while in the public's mind, parole is often something granted by a bunch of soft-hearted kooks appointed by the governor. But there is no question that the jail is a locally administered facility that handles local offenders. Therefore, jail managers have a tremendous potential asset that is denied virtually all other correctional administrators by virtue of location alone, i.e., the possibility of attaining significant credibility with the public and thereby maximizing the use of local resources. This, of course, presumes that the jail manager is competent and thereby worthy of trust. Given that, the very fact that Joe Jones, Jail Warden, lives in a community and as a result has a stake in its well-being gives him a potential status that other corrections personnel rarely attain. If Joe Jones is also the local sheriff, then he has the additional credibility factor of being viewed as the principal keeper of the public safety. If *he* says it is all right to have offenders working in the community on work release, for example, then nay-sayers had better have a few facts to support their arguments rather than relying solely on emotional rhetoric. This is a long way from saying, however, that the local sheriff or jail warden can automatically make any changes in local correctional programming he or she desires; just that the local status makes it easier to sell innovations and reform to the public.

Community-oriented corrections is difficult to initiate in most communities, but the local jail official has a far better chance of beginning these programs than does someone identified with the state or federal bureaucracy. Even where the state or federal government employs someone locally to administer a new concept in corrections, there is still definite suspicion of the anonymous power beyond the community's borders. These distinctions blur in large proportion in many major cities today, where old neighborhood patterns have broken down, civic identity is on the wane, and the increasing mobility of many Americans has served to give a rather faceless coloration to the urban landscape. But in the smaller cities and towns around the nation that have been less effected by changing lifestyles—the communities in which the vast majority of jails are located—zenophobia still exists, and this has been combined with a strident "we won't let it happen here" attitude. Outside the huge cities, one still hears such terms as *outsider* and, disdainfully, *the people from the big city* used with concomitant attitudes of distrust. While television has served to increase the desire for some of the goods and services available in urban America, it has also made people frighteningly aware of urban problems. Surely the most recent national census figures that indicate the incipient start of a reruralization movement will only serve to reinforce such attitudinal structures and beliefs, as people begin searching for identity, roots, and a less complex existence.

In quite blunt terms, using work release as an example, if one lived in a city of 25,000 to 50,000 people or smaller, would he or she be more inclined to support a program that put convicted offenders on the streets for all or part of the day if an official in a position of trust locally advocated the approach as opposed to someone without that local identity? Combine this consideration with the fear, warranted or not, that state or federal control well might mean "dumping" offenders from other areas, even from those dangerous big cities, in the locality, and the question basically will answer itself. With considerable hard work and creativity, state or federal officials might eventually be able to begin a program, but it still would take a near perfect success record and much time before the community would lend support actively to the idea.

If the community will accept the jail as a local institution, then by logical extension the people confined therein are a local problem. Well-conceived public education efforts must stress that crime and crime prevention (including rehabilitation and reintegration of offenders) are decidedly local issues that require solutions tailored to actual conditions within that community. Furthermore, as the police have consciously realized recently, there is only so much that agencies can do to cope with the full dimensions of these issues; effective solutions require the active support and cooperation of citizens. The public will accept the idea that a town or county has some responsibility to solve their own problems in these areas—a somewhat natural tendency that has been reinforced by the disillusionment with lofty, unfulfilled promises made by national and state politicians. Properly and consistently presented, the community will come to acknowledge its inherent responsibility and the negative consequences of continued, passive alignment with the status quo. But this realization pertains only to local problems, and resistance is understandably strong to the transfer of problems by other units of government into someone's territory. Hence, citizens within given jurisdictions can be educated to the point at which they will begin to accept a greater or lesser degree of responsibility not only for local institutions per se but also for the people within them. This is, of course, not universal, since some areas and many citizens will never adopt such a philosophy. However, we will not know what is possible until a genuine attempt is made to increase public understanding of the real problems at hand.

Positive Local Roles for Jails

An increasing number of penologists have become despondent over the possibility of successfully reintegrating offenders who have been isolated in state institutions considerable distances from their homes. This "prisonization" serves to damage or completely abrogate whatever constructive community contacts the person might have had; effectually exiles the individual from the public's consciousness (an extreme example of this being Eskimo villages in the Alaskan bush, where a sentence to state prison has replaced banishment in the local culture to the extent that the community and the prisoner's family refer to him or her, if at all, either in the past tense or as if dead); and returns the offender to freedom as a psychological and physical stranger to his or her environment. The solutions proposed by these correctional authorities tend to fall into two principal categories: first, keep the person, if at all possible, out of an institution initially, i.e., diversion via probation or some other means; and, second, if institutionalized, have the individual participate in as many community-oriented programs as possible, such as work release and furloughs, combined with efforts to bridge the gap between prison and freedom, such as halfway houses located in the community and various early release mechanisms, most notably parole.

Since most offenders spend time in jail at some point in their encounters with the criminal justice process, either awaiting detention prior to trial, awaiting sentencing after conviction or transfer to a state prison, or serving short, misdemeanant sentences, the jail, with its unique ties to the community, is a natural fulchrum for community corrections and a nexus to unite the various entities within the corrections process itself. In other words, the jail provides access to the community and to the offender for the entire spectrum of corrections, should the system choose to take advantage of it.

One argument that is increasingly heard in penological circles is that the state prison systems should assume responsibility for sentenced misdemeanants, thus relegating jails to a purely detention role. However, the theorists advocating such a move fail to recognize several crucial realities in corrections today. The state systems have proved no more effective than jails in successfully rehabilitating or reintegrating offenders. Furthermore, unless the state were to take active control of part of individual jails for the purpose of housing misdemeanant prisoners, these individuals would no doubt wind up in distant, existing state prisons, thereby posing a serious handicap to any genuine attempt at rehabilitation. Given a change in managerial attitude at the jail level, there is no reason why local facilities cannot be demonstrably more effective in reintegrating offenders than the state systems.

The state prison systems have indicated no interest in willingly adding to their own prisoner population counts. Additionally, many state wardens are among the first to mouth the myth that "jails can't do anything with misdemeanants, since they don't have them that long." Such an attitude translated into practice would mean that state institutions would do little more than process misdemeanants in and out of the system. Frankly, unless transfer of misdemeanants were effected immediately after sentencing, a state prison realistically might not have time to do anything else.

A substantial problem would be created by the need to separate misdemeanants from felons in state prisons. Presumably, few, if any, penologists would advocate mixing people, who in many cases would be novices in the crime business and who, by definition, have been convicted of nonserious offenses with hardened prisoners incarcerated for major crimes. With the already overcrowded conditions in many state institutions, adequate separation would be virtually impossible without substantial capital outlay, which, even if the legislatures would finance, would not be ready for approximately five years from the time of appropriation through the bidding, contract award, design, site selection, and construction process. Substantial additions to existing staffing patterns would also have to be secured via the appropriations process—a necessity with success by no means guaranteed.

Some penologists now also argue against the continued local control of jails, pointing out that the political leadership in some counties and cities is not amenable to efforts to secure jail reform. This argument assumes, of course, that a strong case has been made by the jail manager on the local level to improve conditions. Unfortunately, the reverse is more often the truth. Even in those instances in which local officials adamantly refuse to bring the jail operation up to a reasonable standard, two recourses already exist to effect prompt remediation. First, many states have the power via legislation to establish and enforce jail standards. As was pointed out earlier in this book, even when the state has promulgated standards, there is a tendency to hire too few or unqualified jail inspectors for enforcement purposes. There is also the problem of political pressures being brought to bear on any attempt on the part of the inspectors to compel compliance with standards. Nonetheless, if a state government is sincere about improving local jail conditions, a valid, legal mechanism exists by which to overcome staunch, local political opposition, should a governor or state prison system executive care to use it.

Second, succor can be obtained in the courts. Many suits challenging abominable jail conditions have been successful and the courts have mandated specific improvements. Even the most recalcitrant political leader cannot ignore a court order.

Hence, instead of constantly assuming that local officials are almost automatically against jail reform (a possible reflection of an urban bias against rural areas), an intensive effort should be made to educate them to the advantages, both in economic and crime reduction terms, of progressive jail practices. If such an attempt fails and the conditions in the jails warrant, effective, alternate means of rectifying the problem already exist.

If one would assume, then, that the local jail can serve legitimately as a fulchrum for correctional services to the offender, given its location and ties to the community, some or all of the following roles would be appropriate in a coordinated plan for shifting the emphasis of corrections from the state prisons to the community and to actual offender needs.

Diversion

In today's criminal justice universe, diversion programs frequently are located in or immediately adjacent to the courthouse. This is logical, since in most instances formal diversion currently requires official judicial sanction since it occurs after arrest. An exception to this practice would be the police use of citation in lieu of formal arrest in matters of a comparatively minor nature (an extension, fundamentally, of the process used in dispensing traffic tickets to other types of offenses). Hence, diversion takes place during normal business hours, when some staff member is available to gather offender-related information to present to the judge or, as in some programs, rank the offender on a weighted scale that indicates suitability or nonsuitability for diversion. Meanwhile, of course, the arrestee probably spends at least one night in jail (or three, if arrested on a Friday), thus burdening the community with the cost of temporary detention and the individual with substantial inconvenience, at the least. If, for example, the person arrested is also a single parent, a concurrent problem also is raised immediately, which quite possibly will entail additional costs, e.g., temporary housing for the children.

In major cities with court systems functioning at night as well as during the day, a number of alternative solutions to such problems can be developed. However, in the rural areas—where, after all, most jails are located—there is no reason why jails could not play a part in prompt diversion, with benefits accruing both to the community and to the offender. The jail, which functions around-the-clock, could be authorized to administer a suitability scale and be given the power to release on personal recognizance (as could the police). If deemed desirable, a check could first be made by telephone with the local magistrate, justice of the peace, or other appropriate judicial official, or a suitable arrangement could be made for a staff member of the area's diversion program to be on call and to interview the person and gather applicable information promptly at the jail to hasten the diversionary process.

Furthermore, much duplication within the existing system could be eliminated if diversion programs were to make use of the basic information (which could be expanded) now collected by the jail as part of the admissions procedure. By having a staff member report to the jail in advance of the opening of court for the day, a start could be made on verifying whatever pertinent information might be needed to make a reliable diversion decision, instead of waiting to interview individuals at midmorning and then commencing vertification of the information thus obtained. Many rural jurisdictions do not have alternative detention sites, such as police precinct lockups, so the jail would be holding virtually anyone arrested during a particular time span. In fact, there is no reason why the diversion programs cannot have an office at the jail for purposes of obtaining immediate access to potentially eligible people, thereby saving time and needless periods in detention.

Crisis Intervention

Somewhat akin to the need for diversion is that of crisis intervention. Detaining an individual, even overnight, can have serious adverse consequences upon both that person and others in the community, such as family members and employers. What happens to the children when a single parent is incarcerated? If a person is locked up on pay day, how does his wife buy food or pay pressing end-of-the-month bills? As sometimes happens, what occurs when a man from out of the area is detained and his wife is thereby stranded in a strange community with no funds and no one locally to call upon for temporary assistance? All these situations and many more are real concomitants of even temporary detention. The victims in these situations are not the accused, they are perfectly innocent people who now find themselves with definite problems.

One answer is for the jail to assign a staff member(s) to interview all new commitments immediately after admission to determine if any outside problems exist and then to contact the appropriate community resources to provide the needed assistance. Another strategy would be for the most frequently used public and private agencies to assign staff at least part-time to the jail in order to ensure prompt delivery of services. One major new jail still in the planning stages, for example, is considering establishing a group of small offices for agency representatives right next to its admissions area that would be known as a "crisis intervention center." Located in an urban area, the volume of admissions on a daily basis and at somewhat predictable times (people committed to jail by the courts are brought to the jail as a group at about the same time each day) makes this approach eminently feasible, and applicable social service agencies could thus wisely assign staff to cover the peak period.

It is one of the less noted ironies of the justice system that a wholly innocent person can be arrested and detained overnight, released the following day in court, and yet be confronted with serious problems that may take considerable time to resolve upon returning home. People have been fired from jobs for failing to appear without properly notifying employers; they have had their dwellings "cleaned out" by neighborhood thieves who learned of their arrest and realized that no one would be home; they have had their cars impounded; etc. simply because there was no agent of concern to make a simple phone call for them (usually jails allow one call, and for understandable reasons that is very often spent trying to contact a lawyer or bail bondsman). Some provision must be made, hopefully through a concerted, coordinated effort on the part of jail and social service agency officials, to provide an efficient intervention in what for many people is a multiple-crisis situation.

As a perhaps extreme example, one man was frequently arrested and committed to the local jail on Friday nights, having been charged with attempted assault by his wife. Come Sunday night, the wife would drop the charges and the man would go free. He always insisted that the charges were made up by his wife who would then go to a motel and spend the weekend with another man. Finally, out of curiosity aroused by his earnest pleadings that someone at least check to make sure the children were all right, the jail asked the police to check out his story. On Saturday, the police found a young baby covered with its own wastes, a rather hungry three-year-old, and a five-year-old trying to cook for her little brother and sister, totally unattended. A short while later, the police located the mother at a motel with her "lover." Crisis intervention, then, is one of the most needed, yet rarely available, services at any jail.

Court Diagnostic Centers

Undeniably, one of the most critical decisions in the entire criminal justice system is the passing of sentence upon a convicted offender. This judicial determination obviously has tremendous impact upon the individual. But it also is a simultaneous expression of the quality of justice in a given jurisdiction, is viewed by the general populace as a measure of the degree of public safety being provided by the courts, has the potential of reducing or adding to the crime rate depending upon the comparative wisdom of the judge's decision, and has considerable influence upon police morale, among other effects. The sentencing procedure also serves as a determinant of sentenced jail and prison populations. How is this crucial decision made? After all, the convicted person and his or her attorney are only physically present before the court for a few minutes and utter some predictable and often plaintive tale of mitigating factors while seeking the understanding and mercy of the judge. The judge, with very few exceptions, is a former practicing attorney with no special training or proved expertise in the behavioral sciences. Without input from some other source, the sentencing judge must rely on personal experience and play hunches in an effort to balance the needs and desires of the offender and those of the community. Fortunately, a National College of Trial Judges does try to make some training available to the novice jurist; but since a judge is appointed or elected to hear cases, the courses are necessarily of short duration. Certainly nothing in law school prepares the would-be barrister for the eventual "deification" conferred concurrently with the appellation "Your Honor."

Probation agencies assist the judge in arriving at his or her decision on the fate of the offender, in some cases, by preparing a presentence investigation (PSI). This document consists of various items of background information about the person to be sentenced, such as criminal history, family situation, and employment status at the time of and before the arrest. The report normally concludes with a sentence recommendation by the probation officer. It is estimated that in roughly 95 percent of cases in which a PSI is available the judge follows the officer's recommendation.[2] Ironically, someone convicted of a felony has a better chance of coming before the court with such a report in the judge's possession than does a misdemeanant.

The probation officer has the advantage in preparing a PSI of having direct access to the community for purposes of verifying information obtained from the offender and other sources and of interviewing interested parties, such as family, employer, etc. who often can provide valuable insights into the offender's background, personality, and lifestyle. But excessive caseloads, lack of initiative on the part of individual probation workers, a paucity of access to various diagnostic resources, e.g., psychiatrists, doctors, etc., and other similar factors often adversely affect the quality of the PSI. The net result is inadequate input to the judge concerning the sentencing decision and, ultimately, the lowering of the quality of justice within a given jurisdiction.

Logically, there is no reason why jails, working in conjunction with local probation agencies, could not serve as diagnostic centers for the courts. First, many offenders are already in the jail in pretrial and presentence detention status—a fact that guarantees ready access to them. Second, jail staff, as opposed to all other criminal justice personnel, observe an individual 24 hours per day, 7 days per week. Thus, with a modicum of training, staff should be able to contribute poignant insights into the behavior and attitudes of the offender. By contrast, a judge sees the convicted person for only a few minutes at the time of sentencing, and the probation officer's contact is usually limited to the span of a brief interview held during the course of preparing the PSI.

Third, the professional practitioners needed as diagnostic resources for presentence evaluation purposes are the same as those required to staff and administer a balanced rehabilitation program. As so often happens, independently, neither the probation agency nor the court nor the jail could afford to hire such specialists within the strictures of their respectively limited budgets. But jointly, such professionals could be employed, headquartered at the jail, and perform an invaluable service benefiting all three arms of the criminal justice process. Hence, a psychiatrist, doctor, social worker, etc. would be readily available to work in the jail's rehabilitation program, provide sophisticated diagnostic input to the courts, help the probation agency improve the quality of its PSIs, and also make services available to people already on probation.

By combining the probation officer's access to the community with the observations of jail staff and with a professional diagnostic workup, judges would receive markedly improved information (both qualitatively and quantitatively) upon which to base their sentencing decisions, with benefits accruing thereby both to the community and to offenders. In effect, the jail would become the physical fulchrum of a coordinated approach to presentence evaluation of offenders. Such quality diagnoses would also be invaluable to the person or agency eventually given the responsibility for rehabilitation of sentenced individuals.

Tapping Community Resources

Many communities have a veritable plethora of services that are needed by the jail. These include offices of the state employment service, various educational institutions and programs, casework services, and community mental health resources, to name but a few. Most jail budgets would not enable managers to even remotely approximate the range and/or quality of these services if they had to be provided inhouse. Even if such programs could be duplicated within the means provided by appropriated funds, it would be wasteful of taxpayer funds when looked at from a detached, objective perspective.

Of course, the wise use of screened, trained volunteers is one way to build an adequate programmatic base in a facility without an adequate budget. Another is to "borrow" services from other helping agencies in the community. Thus a jail manager might be able to prevail upon the local employment office to provide assistance to inmates nearing their release dates. A mental health center might be able to share the services of a psychiatric social worker, psychologist, or psychiatrist with the jail several hours each week. A school system could provide instructional materials and aides, if not a part-time teacher. The town's bookmobile could make regular stops at the jail, in effect functioning as a quasi-library for the facility or at least to augment the number and variety of reading materials available to the inmates. Similarly, if there is a medical school in the vicinity, arrangements can sometimes be made for the establishment of internships or residencies to be done at the jail, thus increasing significantly the amount of medical coverage.

Other tie-ins with the community are also possible if a little imagination is used. The jail could establish "cottage" industries, for example, by doing envelope-stuffing or other task work for local organizations. This type of activity reduces idleness in the facility and brings the participating inmates some small amount of spending money. Contracts with other public agencies could be negotiated that would provide needed services for less cost than would be possible through the private sector, while simultaneously giving the inmates work and a little income. Washing police cars, doing basic janitorial and maintenance work in public buildings, and maintaining public parks are but several examples of this concept. Many jails already do this type of work, but it is important to build in safeguards to ensure against exploitation of inmate workers and similar abuses. The incident several years ago in which an inmate drowned while being used as a human retriever for a county judge on a hunting trip points up the need for caution in such matters.

With some degree of creativity, the jail can also give service to community agencies. Several facilities use inmate volunteers to establish or augment drug and alcohol education programs in local schools. This type of public service has marked impact and is greeted with appreciation by local officials. Inmate volunteers have also done invaluable work in a number of locales on projects as diverse as building flood control dams, umpiring Little League baseball games, repairing toys at Christmas time, and working with retarded children. The key to the success of such "good neighbor" efforts is to avoid any element of coercion, to encourage inmate participation, and to carefully screen those people from the jail who do get involved, in keeping with the public safety responsiblity and common sense. These activities also benefit prisoners by increasing their self-esteem, utilizing their talents and abilities, and involving them in constructive exercises of responsibility. The good will that accrues to the institution itself can be substantial. A partnership between the jail and the community is thereby established that also serves as a subtle way of changing the stereotyped views about people in confinement.

This approach to jail management requires an intimate knowledge of and involvement in the community. It also mandates aggressive public relations and the ability to both identify resources and convince other agencies to share them. One must maintain a high profile in the community to be effective with such efforts, however; and one must show a willingness to become active in a variety of community causes as a means of establishing and cementing positive relationships and contacts in this area.

Contracting for Services

Because of the vagaries of civil service, the frequent inefficiencies in governmental purchasing procedures, the expenses involved in extensive buying of equipment, and so on, it is sometimes considerably more efficient to purchase services on contract from the private sector than to attempt to provide them from internal resources. Private enterprise often is in a less restricted position to establish proper cost controls on number and types of personnel and the use of materials. Obviously any contract should specify in explicit terms the nature, quality, and quantity of services to be rendered.

As an example of how this contractual concept might work in practice, a look might be taken at an institution's food service program, which is usually a major expenditure of any jail. In addition to providing three wholesome meals a day at a fixed price, a special clause within the contract might stipulate that the food service firm train a given number of inmates in various skills. Once trained, the firm might be obligated to hire some inmates as regular employees within the jail. Thus, in addition to securing an efficient food service operation, the jail would also be creating a useful vocational training program and providing work release opportunities.

Similar contracts could be negotiated with private-sector firms to run laundry, inmate canteen, and various institutional housekeeping functions. Again, the contracts might specify that inmates must be trained and/or employed by the vendors or a cash incentive could be provided to induce the same ends.

Prerelease Function for State Prisons

Given the fact that there are jails in every part of a state and that they have access to local resources and opportunities, they are in a position to perform a prerelease function for state prisoners nearing their release dates. Unless some form of community-based program already exists in the area to which a prisoner eventually will return, state systems could contract with jails to house state prisoners and place them in work release or similar community-oriented programs. The advantages to this approach are that the prisoner is becoming reacculturated to the community which he or she will soon reenter, has an opportunity to renew constructive contacts locally, can pursue realistic planning for postrelease, and can continue in the same job as would be held while on work release status. Such a strategy presumes that the jail meets accepted standards and has an established work release capability. Any contract obviously should reimburse the jail for its actual expenses in making this service available to state inmates as well as ensuring jail officials' participation in the requisite selection process (to prevent "dumping" of prisoners by the state).

While wholly community-based programs established specifically for prerelease purposes is the ideal, it is unrealistic to expect a state prison system to establish such facilities in every community in the state to which prisoners are released. If nothing else, the number of releasees to a particular town, city, or county may be far too small to justify such expenditure of funds and resources. It is especially under such circumstances that a jail-state system cooperative arrangement can fill an urgent correctional need at a cost that would be economical for the state yet not cause a loss for the local unit of government involved. While this concept is hardly new on both the state and federal levels, its use is still not widespread, even though it presents a feasible alternative to the serious prerelease problem.

The Jail Community Itself

While discussion of the potential of significant interaction between the jail and the community is indeed enticing and exciting, the importance of communication within the jail itself must not be overlooked. No matter how dedicated and diligent the jail manager or sheriff may be, it remains for the staff to actually implement any reform measures or improvements. Hence, it becomes important to genuinely solicit input from the entire staff, to keep workers apprised of changes and the reasons for them, and to prepare staff for any alterations in job functions, philosophy, etc. that may be required. Without patient staff involvement and development, confusion and resentment can result that will negate even the best-intentioned efforts at jail reform.

To have any lasting impact, change must be carefully thought out and realistically paced (no organization can accommodate total change overnight). Management's role becomes one of planning, directing, and garnering resources with which to accomplish the desired goals. In other words, the jail manager is the facilitator of change, while staff members are the actual on-line agents of change.

The jail manager should also become familiar with any special skills or talents possessed by individual workers. Sometimes, a correctional officer, for example, may have prior experience or substantial interest in an area of specialization useful to the institution. A woodworking enthusiast might be willing to start a craft shop for inmates, which would thus expand leisure time opportunities for inmates. A ham radio "nut" may be able to improve the communications system within the institution. Recognition and use of such talents also virtually ensures the personal involvement and job satisfaction of the employees in addition to providing services to the facility.

Employees, therefore, should be given ample opportunity to interact with management and made to feel that they are an integral part of the jail's operation, which, in fact, they are. Anonymity frequently equates to indifference, and a jail cannot afford such feelings among its workers. Staff meetings, training opportunities, informal discussions over coffee or during frequent inspection of the institution, and "open door" policies all present management with the opportunity to develop morale and to foster mutual respect and trust—all necessary ingredients in a smoothly operating facility. While sound recruitment practices and ample training are essential elements in creating a good staff, the maintenance of effective management-employee relations is also crucial. Disgruntled employees who are made to feel insignificant within the organization can effectively scuttle the establishment of the kind of intrainstitutional "climate" that is the key to progressive jail operations. All too frequently the well-intentioned reform administrator establishes communication with the inmates and forgets the staff, often with serious adverse repercussions.

It is also imperative to create and maintain communications with the inmate population. This should even go beyond the establishment of a formal grievance procedure. Regular meetings (with staff participation) should be held with inmates to discuss institution problems and to receive suggestions for improvements. Some structure should be given to these meetings so that they do not become gripe sessions, criticize any individual staff member, or constitute a forum for an inmate to lecture on the merits of his legal case or the demerits of his attorney. Written inmate requests should be answered promptly, with a reason given for the particular response. Administrators can place locked boxes in various places within the facility to which only they have the key as another means of enabling the inmates to state their problems. A jail manager may even want to reserve a period of time each week to interview any prisoner who wishes to speak with him or her. However, before initiating action, the wise administrator will fully check out any complaint and take remedial action, if deemed appropriate, *through* the responsible employee to avoid organizational chaos and the possibility of subverting a key staff member.

Choice of the means of establishing communications with both staff and inmates is subject to the individual style of the manager. The important factor is that some constant and consistent channel of communication be made available. Besides making people feel like individuals, access to top administration also facilitates the early identification of problems, so that they may be resolved prior to becoming major crises. Even if people do not like the management response, in most cases they will accept it *if* they feel that they received a fair hearing on the matter. The time to talk is before a major difficulty arises, not after.

Conclusions

A jail is a very definite part of a community that deals with serious and sensitive problems and has a major impact on the quality of life locally. Even if a particular institution had sufficient resources to employ many qualified people and provide numerous programs, the effective reintegration of offenders would still require community participation in the process and a willingness of society to accept its offenders back into its midst. In reality, virtually all jails lack the desired fiscal and personnel resources to do the job and therefore must look to community involvement to supplement them, unless what is desired is a human warehouse that temporarily keeps the problem of crime and its correction out of sight and out of mind.

With creative management that is willing to educate and reach out to the public, the jail has substantial potential as a community resource. While some penologists might argue cogently for increasing use of alternatives to all modes of confinement, the realities of criminal justice in most jurisdictions reflect a frequent use of the jail as a primary tool of the system. The perspective of jail managers must be expanded to identify and tap available local resources, thereby tentatively initiating an active constituency for reform in order to overcome some of the more glaring, traditional limitations of operating such institutions. An approach to jail management that effectually continues to keep the facility hidden from the public is one sure means of perpetuating currently lamentable conditions and intolerable neglect. Wishing for increased support will not make it appear. Resources are available, but they must be actively and aggressively sought and intelligently used. To do so is only to take advantage of the one factor on the jail's side, i.e., local identification.

10 What Can Be Done?

This can't go on; is after all injustice of its kind.

Yevtushenko

You shall not dwell in tombs made by the dead for the living.

Kahlil Gibran

Introduction

In searching for a penological Rosetta stone that would make known suddenly and completely all the answers to the ponderous problems of jails, one is eventually confronted with two stark realizations: first, it is wholly unnecessary to reinvent the wheel; and, second, the most effective solutions are based on readily identifiable basic elements. In other words, if proper classification systems were employed; if more extensive, more effective use were made of a variety of community-oriented programs; if a spectrum of existing human services were made available to inmates; if greater diligence and mere common sense were applied to the creation of an environment more conducive to both staff and inmate safety; if modern management techniques were implemented, among other fundamental improvements that are widely recognized among penologists, jails would become virtually overnight somewhat effective, humane, and efficient societal instrumentalities actively promoting the short- and long-term safety of the public.

One can dream of what would happen if, miraculously, almost unlimited funds would be devoted to the upgrading of jails. In rude reality, very little positive gain would result. For, in truth, huge sums of money have poured into the seemingly bottomless coffers of the criminal justice system through several federal agencies, including the U.S. Department of Justice's Law Enforcement Assistance Administration, and the Departments of Labor and Health, Education and Welfare, among others. The inherent difficulties in letting Uncle Sam do it should be obvious, e.g., bureaucratic inertia, politics, lack of understanding of (and not infrequently outright disdain for) local conditions, fadism and lack of long-term planning, to name but a few. While federal funds have resulted in notable advances in some instances, the overall results (when anyone bothers to find out what they were) do not justify the vast expenditure of tax dollars and the establishment of a monolithic behemoth of a bureaucracy to "administer" them.

The sad fact is that massive expenditures on jails are somewhat akin to performing cosmetic surgery on Idi Amin, i.e., the appearance may change but the basic problem remains. As a very practical example in the jail field, many people in a community obviously and honestly believe that building a new multimillion dollar institution to replace an outmoded, decrepit facility ensures the immediate and permanent resolution of all existing problems. In truth, all too often the same problems persist in the new jail, but in a more contemporary, antiseptic environment. The setting has been improved, but the same antiquated managerial philosophies and techniques used to run the old jail, unless changed, will soon result in a re-creation of the same problems that surfaced in the now-abandoned dungeon. This is not to say, however, that architectural antiques and monstrosities masquerading as jails should not be replaced. Rather, the pouring of concrete and the introduction of new locking systems must be accompanied, in most instances, by a decided change in managerial modalities for a truly new jail to emerge that is free of internal signs of operational decay.

Stripping away all the penological, political, and sociological rhetoric, the solution to the jail problem essentially entails fostering change in two significant groups of people, i.e., the general public and jail personnel. Ultimately, in a democratic society governmental institutions reflect the attitudes of the public. A demonstrated and consistent interest in a particular area of governmental activity by a significant segment of the body politic usually results in some kind of responsive action. Indifference, however, is the best guarantor of the continuance of bureaucratic inertia. Political leaders as a general rule react to constituent pressure, which can merely be an enduring expression of heightening concern by a substantial segment of the voting public. As long as jails remain outside the reward-and-punishment mainstream of political life (good jails mean votes; bad jails contribute to the loss of an election), there is little practical incentive for political leaders to give any serious consideration to the problem.

Even if the necessary level of expressed public concern were to be attained, it would still be necessary to raise markedly the skill level of correctional workers. Of course, increased public interest might well spark higher salary levels, greater status and prestige, and other similar benefits for jail managers and line workers that quite conceivably could attract and retain better qualified personnel. Perhaps such events will have to occur before jails can truly serve to raise the quality of justice within their local communities. But even without the advantages that would accrue from aroused public concern, much can still be accomplished with today's employees if only some proper organization, leadership, and training would be introduced consistently in jails throughout the country. In dealing with human beings and complex human problems, new technologies can only do so much. The ultimate answers depend for their implementation upon competent, dedicated personnel. With such workers, many serious deficiencies in areas like budget and physical plant can be overcome or at least neutralized. Without them, no amount of money or public concern will achieve any noticeable improvement in the state of our nation's jails.

In 1870 the American Prison Association (now the American Correctional Association) adopted a set of principles to guide the administration of prisons in the United States. When those principles were revised in 1970, many observers remarked that if the original principles would only be implemented, surely prisons and prisoners would be much the better for it and revision might be wholly unnecessary. In considering approaches to improve local correctional facilities and detention centers, a similar comment might be appropriate. If we would just put into practice what we now know about correctional administration and human behavior, much discussion about so-called innovative approaches to the problems might be somewhat superfluous. Using this realization as a framework, the rest of this chapter is devoted to suggesting methods of achieving marked and permanent improvement of jails. Very few of these approaches are either unique or particularly innovative; they just are not utilized very frequently, if at all, in contemporary correctional practice.

Suggestions for Improvement

1. *Every jail should establish a coordinated public relations program.* Such an effort should include: giving talks to various civic organizations, church groups, schools, etc.; issuing press releases that emphasize positive accomplishments of the institution, its staff, and inmates (rather than the traditional practice of waiting until the media come calling as the result of some untoward event such as an escape or riot); if feasible within the facility's budget, preparation and dissemination of appropriate written materials describing the jail's operation and philosophy; and the implementation of similar, standard public information techniques. The main purposes for such activity are to let the community know that the jail exists, to make various segments of the citizenry aware of the efforts being undertaken to improve the facility and remedy its problems, and to create an underlying body of residual good will and support for the jail. This is the first step in the development of a supportive constituency in the community.

Most people sometimes tend to form an impression of an institution or agency as a result of contact with one of its representatives. Hence it is imperative that jail staff be reminded frequently of the importance of courtesy in any and all dealings with the general public. The same philosophy holds true for any occasion on which inmates may come in contact with the community, be it as a participant in work release or as part of some other community-oriented program. For those people who at sometime may come in contact with someone associated with the jail, ultimately the most positive statement on behalf of the facility may well be the favorable impression made by a staff member or inmate.

In attempting to foster a positive public concern for the state of the jail, one major problem encountered is that all too frequently the typical citizen fails to take an active interest in an issue unless he or she perceives some direct self-interest. One might even be so bold as to assert that a proved formula for political success (be it for someone seeking election to an office or for a public interest group seeking to arouse active support on a significant scale) is to seek and strike the chord of public self-interest. The public seems to say, "Show how this affects us or we won't get involved".

Ironically, in the case of jails, ultimate benefits to be derived from sound management and progressive operational policies are often rather subtle and long term in nature. For instance, a rehabilitated offender does not receive massive publicity in the press, but rather successfully blends back into the community. People presume that jails will prevent escapes and only show interest when the security system fails. One way to counteract this problem is to demonstrate the cost-effectiveness of rehabilitation and to show graphically how much tax money is saved by a decreased recidivism rate or an effective work release program. Certainly these points can be made via talks and press releases. Heart-warming stories of salvaging the life of a young first offender bring plaudits from various local groups, but saving tax dollars is a fail-safe method of attracting the attention of the local Chamber of Commerce.

Perhaps the most telling point of self-interest, though, is the fact that virtually anyone in a given community can wind up in the local jail. Of course, people without money have a greater chance of remaining in jail than do those of some financial means, but no one is exempt from the possibility of temporary incarceration. Institutions I have personally run have had police officers, elected political officials, a princess, educators, powerful business leaders, professional entertainers—in fact, the whole gamut of society—as temporary or long-term "guests." A person's "out of sight, out of mind" attitude is often changed if that individual can picture himself or herself in such a situation. The key to gaining effective public interest in jail reform is to get people to react to a story in a local newspaper concerning a serious assault in a jail with a "That could have been my kid" instead of a "So what?" or a "You might have expected that of *them*." While it is true that the vast majority of people confined in local detention facilities are members of the lower socioeconomic strata of society, no one group has the exclusive franchise on being incarcerated. When the general public recognizes this fact, active interest in reform will not be far behind. But it is the jail manager who must help in educating the community to the realities of corrections on the local level.

2. *Every jail should utilize volunteers to the greatest extent feasible.* This is one quick, virtually costless way to expand immediately the program services available within a facility. Fortunately, one quite frequent byproduct of an active public relations program is receipt of offers to provide various types of services and assistance from interested private citizens. In addition to waiting and hoping that public relations will result in a number of people interested in volunteering, conscious recruitment can also be done via church groups, civic associations, and other similar public-spirited community organizations. These people can be used in such aspects of institutional programming as education, counseling, leisure services, and library services, to name a few.

What correctional administrators fail to recognize, however, is that in addition to providing needed services within the institution, volunteers also form a base for a potential political constituency supportive of reform efforts. If an individual is so motivated in helping to improve jail conditions that he or she is willing to give up free time and donate services and skills, then that person quite obviously has an active interest in the jail issue. Personal involvement in the operations of the facility solidifies that interest and the person becomes more informed about the problems and identifies with the needs and positive accomplishments of the jail. If the volunteer is at all typical, he or she will discuss the activity with family and friends, thereby, if nothing else, performing a most effective public relations role (an administrator is supposed to promote his or her realm of responsibility, but a private citizen has no perceived personal stake in the matter and, consequently, has more credibility).

By utilizing volunteers, therefore, a facility creates a core of dedicated, concerned citizens with an active interest in the issues of jail improvement. If a person is donating three or four hours a week to providing some service at the jail, that same individual surely will take the time to write a letter to a mayor, city council member, or state legislator on a matter of concern to corrections. No manager in the public sector is going to stay in a position very long if he or she goes around organizing volunteers into picket lines or sit-ins in the mayor's office. Therefore, the use of this new-found power must be exercised subtly, discreetly, and only when absolutely necessary. One actual example of marshaling volunteers for a necessary political purpose should suffice to illustrate this strategem.

A state correctional system had developed a highly specialized and demonstrably successful program that relied quite extensively on the use of volunteers. Faced with a tight budget squeeze, the governor decided not to request money from the legislature to refund the few staff positions entailed in the operation, thereby, in effect, terminating the program. The administrators in the system carefully examined the list of active volunteers and discovered that among other citizens involved were the governor's daughter-in-law, several key financial contributors to the governor's last campaign, and other similar people of influence. They thereupon instructed the staff member running the program to send each of these volunteers a very saccharine letter, thanking them for their devoted services and contributions, and indicating that their services would no longer be necessary because the program was about to end. When the volunteers called to find out some details about the matter, they were very matter-of-factly told that because of the state's budgetary problems, the program had not been included in the budget that had been sent to the legislature. Within five days, a committee representing the volunteers had been formed, traveled to the state capital, and met with the key members of the legislative appropriations committees to express their feelings on the matter. A worthwhile program was saved thereby, and all the correctional officials had done was to be courteous and provide the official explanation issued by the governor's office in response to citizen inquiries.

With creativity and some sophistication of techniques, volunteers can be used effectively to respond to one of the most grievous needs of correctional facilities, i.e., the need for an active, political constituency of substantial influence and standing in the community.

3. *Every state should develop and enforce minimum qualifications and training standards for line and managerial personnel working in jails.* These standards should be realistic and take into account the differing needs, problems, and potentials of institutions located in rural and urban areas. Such a step should ensure a minimum level of staff competency (as defined by the individual states and as reflective of the states' desires relative to jails and the people confined therein) and eliminate or at least substantially curtail some of the more absurd extremes of hiring on a basis of patronage.

Many states already have legal authority to effect some supervision over jails and provide, either directly or indirectly, some portion of the operating funds of local institutions. While mandatory operational standards with strict enforcement procedures are highly desirable, in practice the enforcement aspects become so intertwined with political considerations as to be almost wholly ineffectual. Minimum personnel and training standards, however, are less threatening in nature and easier to enforce, once adopted, and do address a crucial element of jail improvement. Several states are currently preparing such standards.

4. *Where the state prison system operates a training academy or other structured program of preservice and/or inservice training for its own employees, arrangements should be made for jail personnel to participate at nominal or no cost.* Adoption of such a policy would be an inexpensive

means by which states could actively subsidize and improve local jails. Few jails have the fiscal wherewithal or sufficient number of employees to establish an ongoing, structured training program directed by an experienced trainer. For example, if a jail has only 20 employees, it would be very difficult, if not impossible, to create a training regimen that would involve more than two or three employees at a time. Furthermore, hiring of workers is done as vacancies arise, which means that usually only one new employee would be reporting for duty during a particular period. It is unfeasible to establish a full training regimen for one person at a time, so the facility is usually reduced to the expedient of relying on an unsatisfactory method of on-the-job training. Such difficulties can be overcome if local institutions could include their personnel in existing training programs of larger state correctional systems.

5. Every state should give serious consideration to methods of effecting subsidies for jails as a practical means of both upgrading such facilities and providing incentives for communities to undertake improvement of their local institutions. Such a step eventually would also prove to be cost-effective for the state. In fact, an increasing number of states are adopting some form of subsidy program affecting local jails. There is a natural tie-in between state standards and inspection programs and subsidies, in that subsidies could be directly connected with efforts to bring facilities into compliance with jail standards set by the state. Thus, standards combined with some type of assistance to communities to help bring their jails into full compliance could serve to foster a mutually acceptable state-local partnership to achieve marked improvements.

In the mid-1960s, California developed and implemented a concept known as "Probation Subsidy." In brief, the program worked in the following way. A recent average of the annual number of commitments from each county to state prisons was computed and used as a base for determining the amount of any subsequent subsidy. For each person under that base number who was not sent to state prison but handled in some other fashion, such as being placed on probation, the county received a flat payment. The money was given upon the conditions that it had to be used to somehow improve the local probation agency but could not be utilized to increase salaries. In other words, where a county had been sending 1000 people per year to prison prior to the initiation of the subsidy arrangement, if in a succeeding year it sent only 999, it would receive a cash payment from the state; if it sent only 900, it would receive an appropriately larger subsidy. Since the county had to expend the funds so received on improving probation, presumably such services would become more effective, resulting in a further reduction in commitments to state institutions and a larger subsidy in succeeding years for the county.

Without such a program, the counties had little or no practical incentive to put offenders on probation (a county-funded agency and expense) vis-à-vis sentencing them to terms in the state prisons (obviously at state expense). Consequently, the state had been experiencing a tremendous increase in the size of its prison population and was faced with the prospect of spending astronomical amounts of money to build new prisons to alleviate over-crowding. Since probation costs per offender were approximately 10 to 12 times cheaper than prison, the state was saving considerable funds in both the short and long term by effecting a significant subsidy to the counties. It was primarily a failure to provide for demographic shifts in county popula-tions (a major factor in the amount and gravity of crime committed) in the subsidy formula that eventually led to local disenchantment with this ap-proach (e.g., a county could have outstanding probation services and utilize them extensively but, because of a massive increase in its population in the crime-prone age group of 18 to 25, could still be committing more than the base number of people to state prisons, thereby not qualifying for a subsidy).

There are several ways in which subsidies to counties and municipalities for improvement of their jails could be formulated. One would be an outright annual grant based upon the population size of an area, i.e., all jurisdictions with a population under 100,000 would receive so much, those with a population of 100,000 to 250,000 would receive proportionately more, etc. Similarly, the grants could be based on certain specific demographic factors, such as the size of the 18 to 25 age group, or the amount of subsidy could be determined by a combination of demographic denominators and a lessened rate of commitment to state institutions (thereby encouraging local criminal justice officials to handle more criminal matters as misdemeanant rather than felonious and enabling the local jurisdiction to improve its jail to deal with this shift of prisoner population from state to county or city). Another way to accomplish an effective method of subsidization is for the state to assume the costs of providing cer-tain services or to provide the service itself through an existing state agency. Such areas as medical care, education, counseling, and job training lend themselves to this approach. The state might decide to assist in meeting or assume entirely the costs entailed in helping jails make necessary physical plant improvements to bring the facilities up to sanitary, plumbing, elec-trical, and fire code standards. A state could also pay a subsidy to a local jurisdiction for decreasing its commitment rate to correctional facilities, in general, whether they were local jails or state prisons. There are no doubt other formulas by which to effect some form of meaningful state subsidies to local jails.

Several key considerations should be foremost in any discussion of a jail subsidy program. First, the monies given to the local jurisdiction must be used exclusively for the improvement of the jail and should *not* go into the local coffers to be used for any purpose by the city or county officials. Second, there must be some favorable cost tradeoff involved for the state. The first is just plain common sense. If a jail subsidy is being paid, it should obviously not be used to open a new city park or increase the salary of the secretarial pool in the mayor's office. However, there should be sufficient flexibility in the specific conditions attached to the payments that at least some funds can be used, at local option, to establish or expand local services that could be diversionary in nature, i.e., decrease the number of commitments to the jail. For example, if a jurisdiction is still incarcerating people on charges of public drunkenness, the establishment of a detoxification center in lieu of confinement in jail would be an acceptable use of subsidy funds. Such a use would not only benefit the jail but also serve to initiate a needed social service that could begin attacking the problem of alcoholism in the community. The jail is automatically assisted by a reduction in population—in this case a population that it cannot hope to do much to help anyway—and can therefore concentrate its existing resources on the remaining inmates, providing them with more services on an individual basis.

As a practical incentive to the states to undertake a subsidy effort and to ensure that the state receives a return on its subsidy investment, the basis for the formula should include some measure of attaining a favorable cost-effectiveness balance for the state, so that the subsidy program becomes a good fiscal investment rather than a dole. If, for example, as a result of subsidization, fewer people are committed to state prisons, then both immediate (a saving in costs in operating the state prison system) and long-term benefits (with fewer prisoners in the state prisons, the need to build additional, costly institutions is greatly reduced) accrue to the state. Of course, in theoretical terms, any increase in jail efficiency is at least an indirect cost-benefit to the state. For example, if the jail via subsidy is enabled to markedly improve its rehabilitation programs, recidivism should be significantly reduced, thereby also reducing the number of victims who, for instance, will lose fewer days off from work (lost state taxes, loss in gross state product, etc.) recuperating from assaults. In addition, if as a result of subsidy more inmates can participate in work release or after release are able to find and hold constructive employment, the state receives more taxes and increased overall productivity. Hence, some objective, measureable standard of outcome must be developed and utilized as a means of assessing the appropriate type and amount of subsidy to be dispensed. The measurement could be reduction in recidivism, a reduction in the number of commitments to state institutions, increased state taxes paid by work release participants, greater use of diversion programs (demonstrably more cost-efficient and effective than confinement), or some other performance yardstick that would be developed by further, indepth analysis of the topic. For the purposes of the discussion in this chapter, it is the enunciation of the principle that is of primary importance. The actual implementation methodologies must be developed by the individual states to meet their needs and unique local exigencies, i.e., the specifics of a subsidy program that would work in New York might be wholly inappropriate or undesirable in Montana, and vice versa.

6. *Serious consideration should be given to the establishment of regional jails to serve the needs of small, contiguous jurisdictions.* Numerous examples exist throughout the nation of sparsely populated, neighboring counties and towns maintaining separate jails. The problems inherent in such arrangements are obvious: needless duplication of some basic operating costs, budgets (taken separately) too small to provide even a modicum of services (whereas, if combined, they would be adequate to improve conditions and establish some program structure), etc. As has been noted, this situation produces extreme hardship in the case of the unusual prisoner, e.g., a woman. Even if one of these small, rural jails could provide a program or two for men, it could not justify expenditures on services for the few women they might hold other than for the most essential human needs (which, even then, are not always adequately met). While small institutions are highly preferable to huge monoliths in which people are "processed" anonymously, there comes a point at which an institution can also be too small to adequately justify to the public large per capita expenditures for staffing and programmatic purposes.

The regional jail concept has been advocated with varying degrees of fervor within correctional circles for at least the past decade. There are several cautionary notes, however, to be sounded concerning the idea. First, it must be realized that in many suburban and rural jurisdictions, police bring suspects to jail directly rather than initially booking and temporarily detaining them at a precinct house, as is done in large cities. Hence, a regional jail must be so located as not to require extensive travel from any part of the multicounty area served. Unless this location requirement is observed, the police are taken away from their important patrolling function for inordinate periods of time, thus muting their potential effectiveness and substantially reducing, albeit temporarily, their ability to respond in a timely manner to citizen calls for assistance. Second, since the major advantage the jail has over other types of correctional institutions is its location in the offender's community, care must be taken to ensure that a regional jail is conveniently accessible to family, prospective employers, and other constructive community contacts and services. Sometimes a site meeting these qualifications cannot be found, in which case the regional concept might have to be abandoned for that particular area. The various efficiences offered by the regional concept do not override effective police coverage or community involvement (which, after all, is one of the main goals hopefully to be attained via the increased program budget made feasible by regionalization).

7. On an experimental basis, one or more jurisdictions should hire a private-sector, for-profit corporation to manage its jail(s). This is not nearly as farfetched as it might first appear, for several municipalities in this country have hired corporations to provide their police services. There are several rationales underlying this suggestion. First, any contract for such services should include strict performance requirements and provisions for payment based on the production of desired outcomes. If the contractor fails to achieve the results stipulated in the contract, the jurisdiction should simply terminate it. This system would introduce one of the major managerial elements currently lacking in many government services, including corrections, i.e., accountability and payment based on actual productivity and accomplishment. These goals are extremely difficult to achieve under usual governmental operating methods, given the tenured nature of most government jobs, the self-intererst of bureaucrats, and the ability of the bureaucracy at large to avoid managerial techniques that affix accountability and responsibility and attempt to measure accurately the results of policies and programs.

Furthermore, such a free enterprise jail would provide incentives for effective and efficient managerial and line performance. Under current governmental procedures, not counting longevity raises, all employees in a given type of position receive the same remuneration (so-called meritorious raises are either a total joke or insufficient to provide any real incentive). Hence, the manager of an effective jail within a given jurisdiction receives the same pay as someone who runs a wholly substandard facility. The good, efficient, interested line employee gets the same pay as the people who do as little as possible to retain employment. An irony in current practice is that for the good employee to be rewarded, it is necessary to obtain a supervisory position—a different type of job, in essence, at which the person may be no good and in which he or she may be miserable (a prototype example of the "Peter principle" in action). There is no way in practice to reward the line employee as line employee or to differentiate financially between competence and incompetence at any level. Such a situation discourages many people with needed skills and talents from ever entering the corrections field initially and drives others out in understandable disgust and frustration. While being fair to employees, a private enterprise would be under no such restrictions. The corporation actually managing the jail, of course, has the greatest possible incentive for achieving stipulated achievements and standards of operation, i.e., its fee is based on effectiveness, as is continuance and/or renewal of the contract.

Given such stakes, a private enterprise as jail manager also has the incentives to develop new and more efficient ways of achieving desired outcomes. Without such incentives, the jail field does pitiably little research on any aspect of operations, let alone outcome. In fact, it is one of the few "games" in which nobody knows the score and the principal players resist any meaningful attempts to find out. New products, processes, and technologies are developed all the time by private industry with one primary purpose in mind—profit. Apply the same incentive to jail management and one might possibly discover new solutions to old problems. Current jail managers have a decided stake in ensuring that no score is kept. As long as the public does not demand performance data, developing them is potentially threatening to job security. Just keep the lid on, i.e., no serious escapes and no riots, and keep your job. There are no incentives under the present system, except those of ethics and morality, to do the job in any other way, which, apparently for most people, regrettably cannot compete with a guaranteed pay check every two weeks for life. And so the current conditions are perpetuated.

Please do not misunderstand—there are indeed some people in the jail field whose primary motivation is service and whose continued involvement in the work entails considerable financial and personal sacrifice. But for most people, greed appears to be a primary motive for working in jails. It is truly frightening to ponder the kind of people who would work in jails for the money when the salaries are often so pitifully low. Therein lies a simple truth about the whole jail problem. As the old adage goes, "you get what you pay for." In jails, the community doesn't pay much and gets the same. As long as people are going to be working primarily for the money, why not introduce the profit motive and the chance for substantially higher remuneration levels and at least attract greedy people with some talent and ability? The workers with the commendable, service-oriented motivation will stay on and be justly rewarded for their efforts. The employees who will not stay long are those who do not produce, who should not have been there initially.

Before this discussion of the free enterprise jail conjures up images of jail wardens flying off in their personal jets for weekends at their villas on the Riviera, it is necessary to consider the fact that in instances in which such a free-enterprise approach has been taken to the delivery of human services, in most cases the private sector has delivered more and better services to the client at less cost than did the government agency previously in charge of the activity. The reasons for this phenomenon are quite basic. The private-sector manager's "power" is dependent on efficiency and ability to produce profit; the government administrator's power is based on the size of the budget and the number of employees supervised. In other words, to some extent the government administrator's self-interest is best served by the inefficient bloating of personnel and expenditures; the free enterprise manager's, by the ability to maintain costs on the level at which profits will be maximized while still operating at expected norms of efficiency and productivity. Furthermore, private industry is not bound by the cumbersome and inefficient governmental procurement procedures for necessary goods and services. This advantage can also result in significant cost savings. Private concerns also have a tendency to analyze existing problems and design, develop, and implement feasible and efficient solutions as a way of controlling costs and getting the job done better and cheaper. Governmental administrators have little or no incentive to do so.

By the year 2010, when a Japanese conglomerate is running the aid-for-dependent-children program in New York City and a Dutch multinational is in charge of sanitation for Los Angeles, no one will question the idea of a private corporation managing jails. While the concept may be slightly ahead of its time, it is one certainly worthy of an experiment in practice. Certainly few would assert that a private, for-profit organization could do any worse at the task than most cities and counties are doing now.

8. *A computerized classification system should be developed and made available to jails, especially those with inadequate fiscal means and staffing patterns to develop adequate screening systems for themselves.* In an age when sophisticated diagnosis of health problems can be made in situations where the physician is located a substantial distance from the patient, there is no reason why diagnosis of social problems cannot be made using contemporary technology. So many problems plaguing American jails today could be sharply reduced by instituting proper classification programs. Unfortunately, the typical small jail often has neither the means nor the personnel to perform adequately the necessary tasks involved. For instance, it is not at all unusual to find only one employee on duty on a given shift in a jail and, in such circumstances, the person would be responsible for all facets of the jail's operation, i.e., prisoner supervision, booking, and so forth, plus frequently also serving as the radio dispatcher for the sheriff's or police department. Combining the multiplicity of duties with the lack of appropriate training typical of most small jails, it is no wonder that newly committed inmates are assigned to the first empty bed that the jailer sees.

Intriguingly, however, during the usual jail booking process, sufficient information is gathered upon which to base an intelligent initial classification decision for security purposes. By feeding this information into a national computer system, relevant recommendations about the prisoner could be received by the jail employee on duty via terminal before the entire admissions process, i.e., finger-printing, search, and so forth, was completed. Hence, the jailer would be in possession of sufficient information on a timely basis, useful for making a specific housing assignment and other similar decisions. Such a system would also lend itself to making diagnoses for rehabilitation purposes, once the jail would be able to conduct a more indepth interview with the prisoner and gather additional information from the relevant local sources. Such material could again be fed into a computer system with recommendations pertaining to rehabilitation needs eventuating.

Several steps would have to be taken to implement such a computerized classification system. Further research would have to be undertaken to identify and give appropriate weight to those factors most relevant to initial screening and classification decisions. In addition, terminals and other necessary equipment might well be beyond the fiscal capabilities of most jails. Hence, an infusion of federal funds would be required to develop and operate the system. But this type of massive effort has already been achieved in the area of state and national police information systems and there is no reason why the same commitment could not be made regarding jails.

9. *Realistic effectiveness measures for jails should be developed, utilized, and publicized as a means of introducing public accountability into the field as well as for internal management purposes.* Currently no such yardsticks exist by which to determine objectively the effectiveness or efficiency of any correctional institution. True, recidivism studies can be undertaken to show the supposed success or failure of a jail in rehabilitating its inmates. However, recidivism is a rather unsophisticated measurement device, since it fails to take into account comparative degrees of difficulty in successfully rehabilitating various groups of offenders. For example, forgers (many of whom have a serious addiction to either alcohol or drugs) have considerably less favorable prospects for postrelease success than do people in many other offense categories. Similarly, first offenders have a better chance than do hardened career criminals. As a group, people over 40 years old upon release are less likely to return to crime than those in their early or mid-twenties.

Furthermore, there is no universally accepted definition of *recidivism*. Does recidivism mean, for instance, that after release a person is considered a "failure" if he or she is rearrested but not convicted or rearrested and convicted but placed on probation rather than being reincarcerated? Or does a "failure" mean being reincarcerated in the same county or city, the same state, or anywhere in the country? How long must an offender remain crime-free in the community before being counted a "success"? The answers to these and other similar questions would have considerable impact upon any facility's recidivism rate.

Hence, as a means for determining effectiveness of a jail's rehabilitation services (both in absolute and comparative terms), the concept of a recidivism rate needs more careful definition, with a weighting of a variety of variables built into the evaluation process. Even then, once recidivism is accurately determined, one still does not know precisely how or why such an outcome has been achieved (was it education, counseling, or did the offender just get tired of spending every 4th of July in a cell?).

Then there is the question of how to determine a facility's efficiency from a security point of view. When statistics are used at all in a discussion of an institution's security, reference is usually made to the number of escapes occurring within a given year—not even a ratio of escapes to institutional population is used. Obviously the number of escapes by itself says very little. Such factors as age, condition, and design of the physical plant and type of offenders housed therein can have considerable influence upon the number of escapes. Is an escape in which a trusty walks away from a cleaning detail at the county courthouse to be viewed with the same degree of gravity as an escape from within the facility in which a weapon is used? Of course, there are events other than escapes, such as assaults on both inmates and staff and homosexual rapes, that also reflect upon the adequacy of security within a given jail.

A few basic standards do exist and more are being developed relating to such matters as the adequacy of the physical plant and the appropriate numbers and types of staff to be employed per number of prisoners. Organizations such as the American Correctional Association, the National Clearinghouse for Criminal Justice Planning and Architecture, and the Commission on Accreditation for Corrections have been instrumental in the design of such standards. Certainly such devices are helpful in the evaluation of an institution. But compared to the full scope of evaluation needs, the use of these actual and proposed standards, if and when implemented, would be like checking a football field to ensure that it had goal posts and measured 100 yards and that the players had helmets and shoulder pads and then leaving the stadium before the game was played. The former items are necessary for the game to be played at all, but the primary focus of the public and participants most understandably is on the quality of the play and the final score. Unfortunately, too often jails lack the basic equipment necessary to become anything more than inadequate human warehouses; but even in most instances in which proper physical plant and staffing exist, there is no attempt made to determine the end results of the resources and efforts expended.

The current situation is akin to someone managing a business without ever keeping a record of the goods and services produced or keeping a balance sheet to determine profit and loss. Such a businessperson surely would be bankrupt in short order. From efficiency and effectiveness perspectives, jails have been bankrupt for years, but the taxpayers have not demanded an accounting. However, this situation is also a comment upon the abilities and performance of most jail managers. How can anyone be responsible for running any enterprise without wanting to know how well or how poorly such endeavor is achieving its objectives? Without a statement of results, it is impossible to make appropriate improvements within the organization or, for that matter, to be self-congratulatory on a job well done. But presuming that the warden or sheriff is successful in "keeping the lid on" the institution, longevity in the job is virtually assured. Under such circumstances, with no public demand for accountability, the bureaucratic mentality perceives objective evaluation and operational analysis as a threat in far too many cases rather than as a constructive and vital tool of effective management. Many jail officials seemingly have taken literally the advice of that sardonic observer of bureaucracy, James H. Boren, "When in charge, ponder. When in trouble, delegate. When in doubt, mumble."

Since many possible outcome measurements lend themselves to conversion into economic terms, it actually should be possible to construct a profit-and-loss statement for jails. For example, some jurisdictions in the country have developed useful data detailing the specific costs involved in various stages of the criminal justice process, e.g., investigation and apprehension, arraignment, trial, and incarceration. By using or, if necessary, developing such statistics, it is possible to determine how much a recidivist (to use a familiar example of an outcome measurement) actually costs the taxpayers. Conversely, if for the sake of argument one can assume that without proper correctional intervention an inmate will return to crime upon release, then the "profit" or savings accruing to the public from a successful releasee can also be determined. To carry this overly simplified example a step further, some addition and subtraction would then serve to show the "profit" or "loss" produced by the jail in a given year. Although a far greater sophistication of this process would have to occur before the bottom line figures would have any significance, it at least exemplifies various ways in which institutional outcomes and effectiveness can be analyzed and displayed.

In any event, the development and use of effectiveness measures, with results made known to both jail officials and the public and stated in the vernacular rather than obscured in some bureaucratic terminology, would be a major step in advancing public education pertaining to and the management of jails and serve to introduce the concept of accountability on a relevant, objective basis into institutional administration.

10. *Every effort should be made to keep people out of jail who neither need to be nor belong there through greater emphasis on diversion programs and/or changes in either local policy or applicable legislation.* Although this same point has been made elsewhere in this book, it is of such crucial importance that it deserves reemphasis even at the risk of slight repetition. Regrettably, while the jail administrator must cope with the problems of overcrowding and an inadequate resource base to meet the needs of a variety of noncriminal people who often wind up in confinement, e.g., the alcoholic as public intoxicant, he or she virtually is powerless to alter the responsible process. In some cases, anachronistic legislation is the culprit; in others, a somewhat cruel policy of local administrative or political convenience can be blamed, e.g., failure to make proper provisions for the temporary care of neglected and dependent children. As for various diversion strategies possible within the criminal justice system itself, such as release on recognizance or voluntary enrollment in various helping programs providing services rele-

vant to offender needs, their fullest use consonant with the proper regard for public safety is far cheaper and more effective than incarceration in the long run in both economic and human terms.

11. *The Department of Justice should continue and expand its efforts to take appropriate legal action against jails and local officials when violation(s) of inmates' civil rights can be proved.* Recently, the Department, in fact, did initiate cases against three large jails, alleging that various conditions and policies therein served to deprive prisoners of their civil rights. The willingness of the Department of Justice to take some positive steps to afford basic protections to inmates is indeed encouraging. Federal enforcement officials for too long have taken a "hands off" attitude when abominable, shocking conditions in local institutions can be documented. Various civil rights statutes passed by Congress provide requisite statutory authority for intervention, especially in those instances in which responsible local officials refuse to remedy flagrant abuses.

Such a suggestion by no means implies that federal authorities should usurp the authority of units of local government to administer their programs and agencies as they see fit in conformance with perceived local needs and desires. However, when patent neglect or archaic practice results in unconscionable violations of basic human and legal rights, Justice Department officials should exercise their statutory authority in an effort to rectify the problems. Consistent action by the Justice Department in such matters will serve to put jail officials on notice that an "anything goes" method of operation will not go unchallenged. At the same time, the conscientious sheriff or jail warden has nothing to fear, since the Department is only trying to seek effective remediation through the courts in the most extreme instances of abuse. Furthermore, if the Department desired to intervene in a great many situations, local political considerations would provide an effective balance by which to prevent unwarranted intrusion.

12. *The federal government has a legitimate role in effecting jail improvement by encouraging relevant research and by funding general programs of national scope.* While the arbitrary, bureaucratic setting of national standards by the federal government that some individuals advocate would be fraught with severe problems (such as the impossibility of allowing for legitimate variations according to prevailing economic and lifestyle standards in different communities), there are several necessary aspects of jail reform in which the government could be of substantial assistance. There is still a need, for instance, for extensive research on such topics as the actual conditions in jails nationally, offender needs, practical rehabilitation strategies, and many others. As in many of the physical sciences, federal subsidy of such research efforts is fitting and necessary. This is being done to some extent by the Law Enforcement Assistance Administration's National Institute of Law Enforcement and Criminal Justice and the

more recently created National Institute of Corrections. However, to have more of an impact, greater efforts need to be expended on the operational aspects of jail management by researchers with knowledge of the real-world problems of institutional management on the local level.

Within the past year, the National Institute of Corrections has established a National Jail Center in Boulder, Colorado to provide training and technical assistance to jail employees. Potentially, this center could provide a significant service to the field without impinging on local administrative and political autonomy.

Another useful federal effort has been the Law Enforcement Education Program (LEEP), which makes funds available for employees in any area of criminal justice to further their education. Fortunately, this program has narrowly escaped budgetary elimination by Congress on at least two occasions since its inception. As a practical matter, such funds enable progressive wardens, sheriffs and jail employees to utilize community college vocational programs and university courses in various aspects of criminal justice as valuable training mediums and also make possible the upgrading of standards for initial employment. Unfortunately, as a practical matter, the police seem to have made more extensive use of this opportunity than have correctional personnel.

All these programs require an assurance of continuation and expansion, since they make available resources that are beyond the ability of many jurisdictions to provide for themselves. They also respect the uniqueness of different communities, do not represent an oppressive federal compulsion, and are decidedly national in scope. Some, however, could benefit significantly from a closer connection with the actual operational world of jail management in order to ensure their pertinence and enhance their credibility, acceptance, and use by institutional administrators.

13. *A distinct effort should be made to increase the capability of sheriffs to manage jails.* Whether elected law enforcement officials should be responsible for running jails is a somewhat extraneous question. The fact is that 85 percent of jails nationally are administered by sheriffs and will continue to be so for the forseeable future. Because of several factors alluded to in an earlier chapter, e.g., the removal of various policing functions from sheriffs by legislative bodies in some states, thus making the jail the largest part of their duties and power base in a number of jurisdictions, combined with an increasing number of adverse court decisions against sheriffs involving jail conditions, many sheriffs now are expressing a desire to acquire expertise in jail administration. This current climate should be capitalized upon in an attempt to improve the knowledge and skill base of sheriffs. Such efforts could take the form of various types of training opportunities, e.g., a recent federally funded project of the National Sheriffs' Association to revise and update an existing self-study course for jailers. The new

federal National Jail Center is already providing some technical assistance to sheriffs and is trying to develop the capacity to become a national clearinghouse for information on jails and jail management. The National Sheriffs' Association has significant credibility with its approximately 68,000 members, most of whom are sheriffs and deputy sheriffs, and thus could also play a major role in providing leadership, services, information, and materials pertaining to jails to its membership.

Conclusions

There are numerous other valid suggestions that could be made to improve jails. These range from greater involvement of some of the nation's foremost colleges and universities to the hiring of qualified ex-offenders. The preceding ideas are but part of a long list that virtually anyone with concern and experience in the management of jails could develop. Unfortunately the problems are too complex and the number of jails in this country too great for one or even a hundred innovative, dedicated people to resolve on a permanent basis. What these institutions need so desperately are concerned people in every community who are willing to give of themselves to effect answers responsive to local conditions that address the individual needs of offenders. This focus on the offender is really also a realistic expression of concern for the potential next victim of criminal activity. Effective jails, which would actually help to reduce crime through appropriate rehabilitative intervention in the early stages of a criminal career, could impact markedly on the sordid crime scene that exists in almost all parts of the United States.

People apparently feel that crime prevention is solely a police function. They have never been educated to the potential of corrections as a crime reduction force. Maybe the points involved are too subtle to ever have mass appeal. But even the more astute leaders in the police field are now admitting that law enforcement officers can only do so much—to be maximally effective they need not only the moral support of the community, but the active cooperation of a substantial portion of the citizenry.

Perhaps it is easier for the affluent to keep moving further and further away from high-crime areas, but eventually there will be no place further to move and hide. Many people seem to be saying that it is a more viable alternative to pay whatever price is necessary to clutter their residences with security devices, alarms, and sirens; change their lifestyles; and in effect incarcerate themselves in somewhat luxurious quasi-prisons from which they fear to venture forth at night than to get involved in doing what is necessary to assist in improving the criminal justice process. Pity to those people unable to afford such protective trappings.

In the last analysis, one is reminded of the biblical story of Cain and Abel. After murdering his brother, Cain was asked where Abel was. He replied, "Am I my brother's keeper?" In our society, in which tax dollars are being used to lock people away in monolithic, monumentally ineffective institutions, the result of which is additional harm to members of the community, we are all at least indirectly our brothers' keepers. Now what are we going to do about it?

Notes

Chapter 1
Overview of American Jails

1. U.S. Department of Justice, *The Nation's Jails*, Law Enforcement Assistance Administration, National Criminal Justice Information and Statistics Service, Washington, 1975, p. iii.

2. This principle was first enunciated by Howard B. Gill, a distinguished American penologist and criminal justice educator.

3. American Correctional Association, *Manual of Correctional Standards*, Washington, 1966; National Advisory Commission on Criminal Justice Standards and Goals, *Corrections*, Washington, 1973. In 1974 the National Sheriffs' Association, headquartered in Washington, D.C., published a series of seven handbooks that collectively dealt with the major aspects of jail management and operations.

4. The First United Nations Congress on Prevention of Crime and Treatment of Offenders (1955) adopted and approved *The Standard Minimum Rules for Treatment of Offenders* by formal Resolution on August 30, 1955. The General Assembly of the United Nations eventually accepted and endorsed these standards and strongly urged their implementation by member countries via General Assembly Resolutions 2858 (XXVI), December 20, 1971, and 3144 (XXVIII), December 14, 1973.

5. American Bar Association, *World Implementation of the United Nations Standard Minimum Rules for the Treatment of Prisoners* (monograph), Commission on Correctional Facilities and Services, Washington, 1975, p. 18.

6. All statistics cited in the remainder of this chapter, unless specifically noted otherwise, are from *The Nation's Jails*, U.S. Department of Justice, Law Enforcement Assistance Administration, National Criminal Justice Information and Statistics Service, Washington, 1975. This publication is "A report on the census of jails from the 1972 Survey of Inmates of Local Jails" and constitutes the most recent and only reliable source of information available on jails throughout the United States.

7. The source for the material in this section, unless otherwise specifically noted, is the *Survey of Inmates of Local Jails 1972, Advance Report*, U.S. Department of Justice, Law Enforcement Assistance Administration, National Criminal Justice Information Service, Washington, 1974.

8. Ibid., p. 5.

9. American Bar Association, *World Implementation of the United Nations Standard Minimum Rules for the Treatment of Prisoners*, p. 12.

161

10. Neil M. Singer and Virginia B. Wright, "Cost Analysis of Correctional Standards: Institutional-Based Programs and Parole," American Bar Association, Commission on Correctional Facilities and Services, Correctional Economics Center, Washington, 1976, p. 30.

11. Ibid., pp. 76, 82, 86.

12. Ibid., pp. 37, 38.

13. Ibid., p. 18.

14. Ibid., p. 52.

Chapter 2
Components of the Problem

1. In 1972, however, as part of a major reorganization of the structure of its board of directors, the Association amended its bylaws to mandate some representation for short-term institutions and jails. This action was taken at least partially in response to a grass roots effort of the membership to ensure a voice for minorities and various specialist groups in the organization.

2. Model Community Correctional Program, M. Robert Montilla, Director, Report II: Community Organization for Correctional Services," Institute for the Study of Crime and Delinquency, Sacramento, 1969, p. 89.

3. Carl T. Rowan, citing a study by the accounting firm of Coopers and Lybrand as reported by the National Council on Crime and Delinquency, in the *Washington Star*, March 3, 1978.

4. E. Eugene Miller and James E. Murphy, "A Handbook on Jail Programs," National Sheriffs' Association, Washington, 1974, p. 10.

5. Ibid.

6. Howard B. Gill, a distinguished penologist and criminal justice educator, makes frequent use of this expression to describe inappropriate overuse of limited correctional resources.

7. Joint Commission on Correctional Manpower and Training, *The Public Looks at Crime and Correction*, Washington, D.C., February 1968. (The Harris Poll was commissioned by the Commission and published in this monograph.)

Chapter 3
Security

1. Michael Kolinchak, "A Handbook on Jail Administration," National Sheriffs' Association, Washington, 1974, p. 43.

2. National Sheriffs' Association, "A Handbook on Jail Security, Classification, and Discipline," Washington, 1974, p. 53.

3. American Correctional Association, *Manual of Correctional Standards*, Washington, 1966, p. 367.

4. American Correctional Association, *Riots and Disturbances in Correctional Institutions*, Washington, 1970.

5. American Correctional Association, *Manual of Correctional Standards*, p. 369.

6. Ibid., p. 369.

7. Vernon Fox, *Introduction to Corrections* (Englewood Cliffs, N.J.: Prentice-Hall, 1972), p. 157.

Chapter 4
Classification

1. Vernon Fox, *Introduction to Corrections* (Englewood Cliffs, N.J.: Prentice-Hall, 1972), p. 173.

2. U.S. Department of Justice, *The Nation's Jails*, Law Enforcement Assistance Administration, National Criminal Justice Information and Statistics Service, Washington, 1975.

3. Plato, *The Laws*, trans. A.E. Taylor (London: J.M. Dent and Sons, 1960), p. 301.

4. Fox, *Introduction to Corrections*, p. 173.

5. U.S. Bureau of Prisons, *Handbook of Correctional Institution Design and Construction*, Washington, 1949, p. 18.

6. Ibid., p. 18.

7. E. Eugene Miller and M. Robert Montilla, *Corrections in the Community: Success Models in Correctional Reform* (Reston, Va.: Reston Publishing Company, 1977), pp. 153-154.

8. This principle was inimitably enunciated by Howard B. Gill, a distinguished American penologist and criminal justice educator.

9. National Sheriffs' Association, "A Handbook on Jail Security, Classification, and Discipline," Washington, 1974, pp. 33-35.

10. Ibid., p. 36.

11. Ibid., p. 31.

12. *Parks* v. *Ciccone*, 281 F.Supp. 805 (W.D. Mo. 1968).

13. *Seale* v. *Manson*, 326 F.Supp. 1375 (D. Conn. 1971).

14. *Miller* v. *Carson*, 401 F.Supp. 835 (M.D. Fla. 1975).

15. These facts appear in a complaint denoted *Seegers* v. *District of Columbia*, Superior Court, District of Columbia, and were corroborated by press reports of the incident. This case was settled recently out of court.

16. *Rhem* v. *Malcolm*, 396 F.Supp. 1195 (S.D.N.Y. 1975).

Chapter 5
How to Inaugurate Programs Now

1. *Time*, June 30, 1975, p. 18, cites a report by Gregory Krohm of the Virginia Polytechnic Institute's Center for the Study of Public Choice.

Chapter 7
Work, Training, and Study Release

1. This term was coined by the late Donald R. Clemmer, noted American penologist and correctional administrator.

2. U.S. Department of Justice, *The Nation's Jails*, Law Enforcement Assistance Administration, National Criminal Justice Information and Statistics Service, Washington, 1975.

3. E. Eugene Miller and M. Robert Montilla, *Corrections in the Community: Success Models in Correctional Reform* (Reston, Va.: Reston Publishing Co., 1977), p. 186.

4. Ibid., pp. 186-187.

5. Walter H. Busher, *Ordering Time to Serve Prisoners: A Manual for the Planning and Administering for Work Release* (Sacramento: American Justice Institute, 1973), p. ix.

6. Dean V. Babst, *Day Parole and Employment of County Jail Inmates, 1960 Survey of Wisconsin's Huber Law*, State Department of Public Welfare, Bureau of Research, Research Bulletin C-6, Madison, February 1962.

7. Alvin Rudoff and T.C. Eccelstyn, *Jail Inmates at Work* (San Jose, Calif.: San Jose College Foundation, 1971).

8. Miller and Montilla, *Corrections in the Community*, p. 199.

9. Mason J. Sacks, "Making Work Release Work: Convincing the Employer," *Crime and Delinquency*, 21, no. 3 (July 1975):255-265.

10. E. Eugene Miller and James E. Murphy, "A Handbook on Jail Programs," National Sheriffs' Association, Washington, 1974, p. 35.

Chapter 8
The Legal Rights of Prisoners

1. *Robinson* v. *California*, 370 U.S. 660 (1962).

2. Many of the cases cited in this section emanated from prisons, not jails. Since the rights involved and conditions of confinement, however, are quite similar, if not identical, to those impacting jails, it is a reasonable assumption that these precedents and judicially ordained requirements also, by extension, apply to jails as well.

3. *Landman* v. *Peyton*, 370 F.2d 135 (4th Cir. 1966): *Holt* v. *Sarver*, 309 F.Supp. 362 (E.D. Ark. 1970), *Aff'd*. 422 F.2d 304 (8th Cir. 1971); *Howard* v. *Smyth*, 365 F.2d 428 (4th Cir. 1966), *cert. denied*, 385 U.S. 988 (1966); *Sinclair* v. *Henderson*, 331 F.Supp. 1123 (E.D. La. 1971); *Young* v. *Wainwright*, 499 F.2d 388 (5th Cir. 1971).

4. *Howard* v. *State*, 28 Ariz.Rpt. 433, 237 P.203 (1925); *Dabney* v.

Cunningham, 317 F.Supp. 57 (E.D. Va. 1970); *Kritshy* v. *McGinnis*, 313 F.Supp. 1247 (N.D. N.Y. 1970).

5. *Burns* v. *Swenson*, 430 F.2d 771 (8th Cir. 1970); *Smoake* v. *Fritz*, 320 F.Supp. 609 (S.D. N.Y. 1970); *Landman* v. *Royster*, 333 F.Supp. 621 (E.D. Va. 1971).

6. *Landman* v. *Peyton*, 370 F.2d 135 (4th Cir. 1966).

7. *Dillard* v. *Pitchess*, 399 F.Supp. 1225 (C.D. Calif. 1975).

8. *Milburn* v. *Fogg*, 393 F.Supp. 1164 (S.D. N.Y. 1975).

9. *Wolff* v. *McDonnell*, 418 U.S. 539.

10. *Miller* v. *Carson*, 401 F.Supp. 835 (M.D. Fla. 1975).

11. *Baxter* v. *Palmigiano*, 74-1187 U.S.Sup.Ct. 1976.

12. *Carlo* v. *Gunter*, 520 F.2d 1293 (1st Cir. 1975); *Davenport* v. *Howard*, 398 F.Supp. 376 (E.D. Va. 1974); *Cardaropoli* v. *Norton*, 523 F.2d 990 (2nd Cir. 1975).

13. *Trop* v. *Dulles*, 365 U.S. 86 (1958).

14. *Weems* v. *United States*, 217 U.S. 349, 373 (1910).

15. *Wilkinson* v. *Utah*, 99 U.S. 130, 136 (1878).

16. *Jackson* v. *Bishop*, 404 F.2d 571 (8th Cir. 1968).

17. *Landman* v. *Royster*, 333 F.Supp. 621 (E.D. Va. 1971).

18. *Foster* v. *Jacob*, 297 F.Supp. 299 (C.D. Ca. 1969).

19. *Konisberg* v. *Ciccone*, 285 F.Supp. 585 (W.D. Md. 1968); *Aff'd.*, 417 F.2d 161 (8th Cir. 1969).

20. South Carolina Department of Corrections, *The Emerging Rights of the Confined*, Columbia, 1972, p. 119.

21. Ibid., pp. 113, 114.

22. Ibid., p. 119.

23. *Wright* v. *McMann*, 321 F.Supp. 127 (N.D. N.Y. 1970).

24. *Jordan* v. *Fitzharris*, 257 F.Supp. 674 (N.D. Cal. 1966).

25. *Landman* v. *Royster*, 333 F.Supp. 621 (E.D. Va. 1971).

26. *Barnet* v. *Rodgers*, 410 F. 2d 995 (D.C. Cir. 1969), is but one of many cases on this point.

27. *Bloeth* v. *Montanye*, 514 F.2d 1192 (2nd Cir. 1975); *Cassidy* v. *Blalock*, 392 F.Supp. 335 (W.D. Va. 1975).

28. *Miller* v. *Carson*, 392 F.Supp. 515 (M.D. Fla. 1975).

29. *Rhem* v. *Malcolm*, 389 F.Supp. 964 (S.D.N.Y. 1975); also *Miller* v. *Carson*, 392 F.Supp. 515 (M.D. Fla. 1975).

30. *Rhem* v. *Malcolm*, 396 F.Supp. 1195 (S.D.N.Y. 1975).

31. *Costello* v. *Wainwright*, 397 F.Supp. 2d (N.D. Fla. 1975); *Dillard* v. *Pitchess*, 399 F.Supp. 1225 (C.D. Calif. 1975); *Shannon* v. *Lester*, 519 F.2d 76 (6th Cir. 1975).

32. *Miller* v. *Carson*, 392 F.Supp. 515 (M.D. Fla. 1975).

33. *Hampe* v. *Hogan*, 388 F.Supp. 13 (M.D. Pa. 1974); *Mason* v. *Ciccone*, 517 F.2d 73 (8th Cir. 1975); *Ray* v. *Parrish*, 399 F.Supp. 775 (E.D.

Va. 1975); *Gibson* v. *Charlottesville-Albemarle Joint Security Complex*, 401 F.Supp. 544 (W.D. Va. 1975); *Wiggins* v. *Anderson*, 386 F.Supp. 369 (E.D. Okla. 1974).

34. *Cudnick* v. *Krieger*, 392 F.2d 305 (N.D. Ohio 1974).

35. *Rhem* v. *Malcolm*, 507 F.2d 333 (2nd Cir. 1974).

36. *Cogle* v. *Ciccone*, 308 F.Supp. 1122 (W.D. Md. 1969).

37. *Rowland* v. *Sigler*, 327 F.Supp. 821 (D. Neb. 1971).

38. *Brooks* v. *Wainwright*, 428 F.2d 652 (5th Cir. 1970); *Winsby* v. *Walsh*, 321 F.Supp. 523 (C.D. Cal. 1971).

39. *Seale* v. *Manson*, 326 F.Supp. 1375 (D. Conn. 1971).

40. *Crowe* v. *Erickson*, 17 Crim. L. Rptr. 2093 (D.S.D. 1975); *Teterud* v. *Burns*, 522 F.2d 357 (8th Cir. 1975); *Teterud* v. *Gillman*, 385 F.Supp. 153 (S.D. Iowa 1974).

41. *Miller* v. *Carson*, 392 F.Supp. 515 (M.D. Fla. 1975); *McCray* v. *Burrell*, 516 F.2d 357 (4th Cir. 1975).

42. *Miller* v. *Carson*, 392 F.Supp. 515 (M.D. Fla. 1975).

43. Ibid.

44. *Bel* v. *Hall*, 392 F.Supp. 274 (D. Mass. 1975).

45. *Miller* v. *Carson*, 392 F.Supp. 515 (M.D. Fla. 1975).

46. *Bel* v. *Hall*, 392 F.Supp. 274 (D. Mass. 1975).

47. *Nelson* v. *Bishop*, 390 F.Supp. 1191 (E.D. Tenn. 1974); *Burke* v. *Levi*, 391 F.Supp. 186 (E.D. Va. 1975).

48. *Stone* v. *Schmidt*, 398 F.Supp. 768 (W.D. Wis. 1975); *Finney* v. *Arkansas Bd. of Corrections*, 505 F.2d 194 (5th Cir. 1974).

49. 390 F.Supp. 482 (N.D. Miss. 1975).

50. *Russell* v. *Oliver*, 392 F.Supp. 470 (W.D. Va. 1975); *Paka* v. *Manson*, 387 F.Supp. 111 (D. Conn. 1974).

51. 509 F.2d 1405 (4th Cir. 1975).

52. *Miller* v. *Carson*, 392 F.Supp. 515 (M.D. Fla. 1975); *Rhem* v. *Malcolm*, 507 F.2d 333 (2nd Cir. 1974). *Dillard* v. *Pitchess*, 399 F.Supp. 1225 (C.D. Calif. 1975).

53. *Rhem* v. *Malcolm*, 389 F.Supp. 964 (S.D. N.Y. 1975).

54. *McCray* v. *Sullivan*, 509 F.2d 1332 (5th Cir. 1975).

55. *State* v. *Colby*, 210 S.E.2d 914 (Sup. G. S.C. 1975).

56. U.S., 97 Sup.Ct.1491, April 27, 1977.

57. *Brown* v. *Pitchess*, 119 Cal.Rptr. 204 (Sup. G. Calif., 1975); *Cruz* v. *Hauck*, 515 F.2d 322 (5th Cir. 1975); *Gaglie* v. *Ulibarri* 507 F.2d 721 (9th Cir. 1974); *Miller* v. *Carson*, 392 F.Supp. 515 (M.D. Fla. 1975).

58. *Coleman* v. *Peyton*, 302 F.2d 905 (4th Cir. 1966).

59. 393 U.S. 483 (1969).

60. South Carolina Department of Corrections, *Emerging Rights of the Confined*, p. 54.

61. *In re Harrell*, 87 Cal.Rptr. 504, 470 P.20 640 (1970).

62. *People* v. *Harmon*, 232 N.W. 2d 187 (Sup. Ct. Mich. 1975); *People* v. *Luther*, 232 N.W. 2d 184 (Sup. Ct. Mich. 1975); *People* v. *Lovercamp*, 118 Cal.Rptr. 110 (Ct. App. Calif. 1974).

63. *Holt* v. *Sarver*, 300 F.Supp. 362 (E.D. Ark. 1970).

64. 252 F.Supp. 679 (N.D. Ga. 1966).

65. *Holt* v. *Sarver*, 300 F.Supp. 362 (E.D. Ark. 1970).

66. South Carolina Department of Corrections, *Emerging Rights of the Confined*, p. 137.

67. *Jones* v. *Wittenberg*, 330 F.Supp. 707 (N.D. Ohio 1971); *Hamilton* v. *Love*, 328 F.Supp. 1182 (E.D. Ark. 1971).

68. *Irwin* v. *Arrendale*, 117 Ga.App. 1, 4, 159 S.E. 2d 719, 722 (1967).

69. *Adams* v. *District of Columbia; see Washington Post*, December 11, 1976 for a summary of the case and of the trial. It should be noted that the litigants eventually reached an out-of-court settlement for a far lower (though still substantial) cash figure than that originally awarded by the jury.

70. *John Doe* v. *Swinson; see Washington Star*, September 4, 1976 for a summary of the case and of the trial. The amount actually received by the plaintiff was eventually lowered via an out-of-court settlement between the litigants.

71. American Correctional Association, *Legal Responsibility & Authority of Correctional Officers*, College Park, Md., 1975.

72. Various conversations with staff in different jails and prisons throughout the country.

73. For an excellent discussion of the entire correctional labor movement, see M.R. Montilla, *Prison Employee Unionism: A Management Guide for Corrections Administrators* (Sacramento: American Justice Institute, 1977).

74. Excerpt from a private conversation with an experienced jail warden about the changing law of corrections.

Chapter 9
The Jail's Role in Community Corrections

1. During the course of a consulting engagement in Colorado, I analyzed this situation and recommended appropriate alternative resolutions.

2. Vernon Fox, *Introduction to Corrections*, (Englewood Cliffs, N.J.: Prentice-Hall, Inc., 1972), p. 109.

About the Author

E. Eugene Miller has had significant experience in the operation of local jails. He began his career as a volunteer at the Bucks County (Pa.) Prison, which is nationally known for its innovative approaches to dealing with short-term offenders. As superintendent of the Women's Detention Center in Washington, D.C. and, later, as correctional facilities administrator for the State of Alaska, Mr. Miller inaugurated a variety of new and successful offender programs and managerial techniques, many with a decidedly community orientation.

Mr. Miller is currently a Washington-based corrections consultant, providing a wide range of services to governmental agencies, private organizations, architectural firms, and attorneys. In addition, he is an adjunct member of the faculty of American University's Center for the Administration of Justice. His articles have appeared in the leading correctional journals, and he is the coauthor of a textbook entitled *Corrections in the Community: Success Models in Correctional Reform*. Mr. Miller is also active in several professional organizations and is a former member of the Boards of Directors of the National Jail Association and the Western Correctional Association. In 1976 and 1978 he was selected as one of the Outstanding Young Men of America.